Weathered Roots
*A Memoir of Recaptured Meals and
Memories from the 1900's Moving Forward*

by Vickie Owens

Copyright © 2016 by Vickie Owens
All rights reserved.

Book cover by Illustrator H. N. Sieverding

All rights reserved. This book, or parts thereof,
may not be reproduced in any form without permission.
Author is not responsible for any or all allergies that may occur
during the use of any recipe therein.

Vickie Owens
at
Weatheredroots60@gmail.com

ISBN 13:978-1537447469
ISBN-10:1537447467

Printed in the United States of America

I Dedicate This Book To

My Grandson, Ryan Elliott
Who inspired me to write again
He believed in me

To My Children
Kristie, Chad and Sean

To My Grandchildren
Ryan, Mary, Myra, Wyatt and Scarlett

To My Rock
Roy (Punk) Davis
B: 10/25/1956 D: 8/03/2015

To My Grandparents
Lillian and Charley Davis
Who made this possible

Acknowledgements

I would like to thank Sandy Heth, the granddaughter of Charley and Lillian Davis for her hard work and dedication to this book. Her editing skills and word style helped bring this book alive.

Thank you Susan Cantine-Maxson, my college Literature Instructor for taking the time to do a final edit, and for your kind words and wonderful advice.

To Fred and Ellen Phelps of Colesburg, Iowa, thank you for the additional recipes.

To my cousin, Barb Kramer Flores, you were a great help, even though you were tucked away in Afghanistan, I appreciated your input.

To my critiques, Jean Ben, Julie Spillane, Jennifer Kennedy, and Julie Davis...Thank you!

Contents

Life at the Old Log Cabin	3
Recipes	19
Vickie's Poetry	247
Pictures	269
Log Cabin Kids	287
Miscellaneous Pictures, Newspaper Clippings, Stories	291
Charles Button Davis-Sea Captain	311
Genealogy	323
The Final Journey	343

Preface

What feels like miles from the world's center, nestled deep in the woods on ten acres of rolling hills stretching out to the sky, stands a four-room log cabin surrounded by knee high waving grasses and thick graceful pines whispering in the wind. Towering oak trees stand stern and eternal, their leaves in a constant state of change with the seasons. Fall is the grandest season of all. The leaves on the trees turn a golden bronze, with a tad bit of rust shining through. The red from the maples turns the hillside ablaze! My eyes continue to roam the brilliant autumnfest of color; it appears picturesque, as if emerging out from an artist's brush.

The Little Turkey River weaves its way through the rich bottom land. Trout sometimes pop their heads above the rivulets as if to say, "Get your cane fishing pole, you should be fishing on this bright, warm, sunny day!" I continue to follow the woods north along the creek line, admiring the minutiae of nature's beauty; ferns moss, water cress, and the precious, delicate lilies of the valley sprouting from underneath the distant trees. I reach a dead end and see an opening in the hillside, water is flowing down from far above. I am amazed! Before me is the most alluring little waterfall I have ever seen. I reach out and let the water flow over my hands. It is crisp, cold and clean, as it trickles down over the ancient igneous rocks. Sunbeams pierce through the forest canopy sending shards of bright light streaming down from heaven above. The sun's rays appear like shimmering Angels shining their light on me. This day lives eternal in my memory. Nature and its rich grandeur blooms right before my eyes. I will cherish this moment now and through all the days of my life.

These are my hills, my people and my roots. I am the sparkling green-eyed granddaughter of wonderful grandparents who lived a simple, harmonious life in these backwoods and this is my memoir, "*Weathered Roots*." Within its pages are many adventures, pictures, poetry, recipes, short stories and genealogy. I hope you enjoy this journey with me.

Vickie Owens

Life at the Old Log Cabin

The trip to the back hills of Colesburg, Iowa, felt like an eternity for a young girl, but it was only twenty-six miles from our Dubuque home to Grandma Lillian and Grandpa Charley Davis' Old Log Cabin. It was a Sunday ritual from cool, early spring days until the end of fall. Every Sunday morning, we loaded the car with essentials Grandma and Grandpa might need for the week ahead. My journey began in the late 1950's, and I don't know if it will ever end.

Dad drove his old white station wagon straight north on Highway 52 & 3 out of Dubuque. With childish impatience, I often wished the trip was over before it began. I counted winding road curves along the way, and when I lost count of the curves, I stuck my little nose out the window to sniff the sweet country air and count farms as each one passed by. On rainy days, I traced the raindrops with my tiny fingertips as they streamed down the car windows. The trip didn't seem as long when I managed to keep my busy mind occupied with other things.

Gillespie Hill loomed ahead; it was an adventurous seven-tenths of a mile-long thrill ride on the highway that climbed up the east side of a limestone cliff. One tight treacherous curve followed another. It felt like a tilt-a-whirl. My scared, tiny body swayed back and forth in the back seat as we wound each curve, the next tighter than the last. I felt dizzy when we arrived at the top of this dreadful climb, but now, only seventeen more miles remained.

There it is! Holy Trinity Catholic Church. Its towering spires stretching straight up. Luxemburg at last. This was my happy place! Three miles to go before we turn right on to crunching gravel that lead to the top of the lane to the Old Log Cabin. It wasn't much of a lane, more like a path; a three quarter mile one at that, surrounded by dense woods.

With each step dried old branches crackled under foot, and the tallest pines sang a soft melody on cool breezes. Honeysuckles grew in abundance and wild daisies begged to be picked. On dreary days with the forest hidden in a mist, I felt like Little Red Riding Hood, often believing that the Big Bad Wolf was lurking behind a tree smacking his lips, waiting for a tasty tidbit of a curious child like me. My imagination ran wild!

Sometimes, on wet days I wished we would have walked to the cabin upward through *"The Bottom."* The bottom land was on the south side of the cabin. If we walked the bottom, it meant we had to travel into Colesburg, which required an additional 3 ½ mile drive along Hwy 3, but then we avoided the path through the woods. The bottom was flat in all directions; no Big Bad Wolf lurking in the trees. The big difference between the wooded approach and the bottom land was the Little Turkey River that had to be crossed; either was an adventure.

Prior to our trip, if it rained heavily, the Little Turkey washed up and out of its banks and made it more dangerous for those on foot. Occasionally, the river flooded. This brought back memories about the death of my Great Grandmother, Mary Angel Cole; Lillian Davis' mother. Mary refused to leave her cabin during a heavy down pour and was swept away in the raging waters of the Little Turkey River in 1925. Her body was found near Millville, IA with her hair tangled around branches floating in the river.

As a young child, my heart was captivated by my grandma and grandpa's primitive lifestyle. This remains true today. Every thought that passes through my mind about the Old Log Cabin brings a rush of long ago, and weathered roots of my past. Everything comes alive! I sense its presence. I feel its breath pass through me. I visualize the roaming hills with tall oak, walnut and majestic pine trees. The lilies of the valley send off a sweet aroma from their delicate, bell-shaped blossoms. The spectacular waterfall tumbles down its hillside like a wall of blue satin streaming into a varnish clear pool at the bottom. I look into the water and my reflection, luminescent on the surface, appears like that of an angel.

But the air contains other human made scents as well— Grandma's fresh homemade bread, the sweet aroma of gooseberry pie being baked in the woodstove oven. A fresh side of pork sizzles in the old rustic iron skillet. My memories hang upon these fragrances, never to be forgotten. After all, wasn't it just yesterday?

The Old Log Cabin on its ten acres was a place of love, hard work, dedication, family, and a place of rest. My Grandma and Grandpa Davis met not far from these ten acres, fell in love, and married. Over the years their love grew into a family of nine children: (Fannie, b: 1915, Merle, b: '17 Mary, b: '20, Roy, b: '22, Clarence, b: '24, Minnie, b: '25, Dorothy, b: '29, Cletus, b: '32, and Virginia, b: 1934). Today all have passed, except for Minnie. She is 91 years old and proven to be one strong Davis pioneer woman.

In my mind's eye, Grandpa Charley was a giant of a man; tall, stern, with deep set steely eyes, and his snow white hair was always perfectly combed, not a strand out of place. He looked sophisticated at times, but his shabby bib overalls with turned up pant legs and his worn out work shoes proved he labored hard every day. Grandpa could also be strict and stern; hard as stone. His actions spoke louder than words. When his kids didn't listen he grabbed a willow branch off the closest tree and used it to teach a bitter lesson. He spoke few words, but the kids knew each word meant business.

His sternness and perseverance allowed him to provide for his family with hard work and dedication to his ten acres. He built their four-room log cabin from surrounding timber. He cut tall, straight, walnut and oak trees the day long, dragging each log out of the woods toward its destination. He was determined to build a place a family could call home, "The Old Log Cabin." Not much by today's standards, but for Charley and Lillian, it was everything, and for me, it was my escape, my bit of heaven on earth.

The downstairs of the cabin consisted of two rooms -- the kitchen and my grandparent's bedroom. The kitchen floors were hewn from unfinished timber. The walls were lined with old newspaper, *comics and all*, for decorative purposes, but mostly for insulation to keep out the harsh cold winds in the dark of winter. We read the walls, over and over again. An iron cook stove heated the entire house and allowed grandma to cook and bake many fine meals. Grandma had no problem firing up the stove. She said, "The magic of the heat is in the hardness of the wood." A rickety wooden table with equally old wooden chairs sat centered between the two kitchen windows.

Grandma made flour-sack curtains to hang over the windows. A kerosene lantern centered on the table, provided the light for the room. A five-gallon metal bucket filled with fresh, cold, spring water and covered over with protective cheese cloth sat on another small wooden table in the corner. A chipped porcelain long-handled ladle was used for dipping for a drink, and it hung from a nail on the wall. Spring water always tasted cold, fresh, and so good.

Each morning, Grandma trekked up the hillside and filled her bucket with fresh spring water that bubbled out of the ground. Some days she made several trips, depending on how much water she needed for cooking, or anticipated company. She always made certain she had enough left for drinking. Eight hard-working kids drank gallons of this fresh water to keep hydrated through the course of long, hot, hard-working days.

Their ice-box was a root-cellar cut into the hillside with a deep set door to keep cold air inside. In mid-winter, Grandpa would go down to the creek and remove ice blocks to line the cellar walls. He spread sawdust on the ice blocks. This method prevented ice from melting too quickly and kept food preserved throughout the coming seasons.

My grandparents slept in a small room directly off the kitchen. An old iron bed with creaking coil springs and feather-tick mattress was the only furniture in the room. The bed was covered with a homemade quilt cut from left over fabric and feather tick pillows were made by Grandma's capable gracious hands. There were no closets to speak of; what clothes they owned hung from hooks or nails pounded into the walls.

On the opposite side of the kitchen were steep, rough, wooden steps that led up to the children's bedrooms. The ceiling was made of slanted logs. Each room had a single window for sunlight to shine through in the morning, and for young dreamers to wish upon a star come night. With an open floor plan, each bedroom flowed into the next. The second bedroom mirrored the first. The children's clothes hung from hooks pounded in the wall. Each room had two iron beds with squeaky coil springs, feather tick mattresses and pillows, and heavy quilts were folded neatly and draped across the bottom of each bed. At bedtime, the kids hung their clothes on the hooks, and their shoes were neatly lined up along the bottom of each bed.

Downstairs a thick wooden latch kept the front door shut

and secure. Wooden hooks were pounded into the wall next to the door and served as a place to hang coats and hats.

Outside, away from the front door, stood the OUTHOUSE, a *two-seater*. I laughed at the thought of pooping being a "him and her" experience, or just maybe the family that pooped together, stayed together. All the nieces and nephews joked about it. As a city raised kid, that OUTHOUSE scared me! My early experience using it was not pleasant. I was certain I would fall in the hole and emerge covered head to toe with human manure! I begged to pee in the woods, but my folks did not consider that ladylike. Why was an outhouse lady like? It seemed primitive to me.

No one went to the OUTHOUSE without taking Grandma's Walking Stick. I didn't understand why until I was told that the stick was used for tossing BLACK SNAKES out of our way. SNAKES!!! The slithery creatures hung out in the OUTHOUSE to eat INSECTS AND RODENTS!!! MICE!!! When I saw that snake, I snagged it with the stick, flung it out the door! This made me want to pee in the woods even more, or maybe just go home. Another thing I hated about that terrible place was the SPIDERS!!! I watched them dance in their webs, rolling up flies for their warm snacks. I could barely concentrate on my duty. Yes, the outhouse was my worst nightmare while visiting.

The woodshed also sat a short distance below the cabin. Grandpa, the tall, strong man that he was, always made sure it was stacked full before the start of Iowa's long, blustery winter months. In the fall of the year he worked long hours so he would have plenty of wood ready for the icy cold season ahead. His calloused hands and worn saw and buck-saw blades were proof that this chore never went undone.

Grandpa also worked for farmers in the surrounding area. He plowed and harvested for extra cash whenever the opportunity presented itself. He hunted wild ginseng from his ten acres. Ginseng grows in shaded, wooded areas where it stays cool from September through December. He was an experienced ginseng hunter, knowing exactly where to look. The green leaves were camouflaged by other green leaves growing next to it. It could easily be mistaken. When he had harvested enough, he brought the raw plants home to Grandma. Grandma knew everything about ginseng. She understood it was delicate and used for herbal remedies. She handled it carefully, washing it first, and then hung it to dry in the kitchen. In cooler weather, Grandma would hang it for about two weeks in the kitchen warmth. When it was properly prepared, Grandpa took it to Colesburg and sold it. He also hunted for agate; a cash-worthy rock.

Grandpa was very sneaky about cooking up his moonshine. White Lightning! The still was hidden deep in the hillside, not to be found. He only ventured into the woods at nightfall so he couldn't be followed. He would get drunker than a proverbial skunk before coming out of the woods. Relatives and close-knit neighbors loved his moonshine. It was said, "The government came after Grandpa Charley one day, but they never found his stills."

In winter, Grandpa trapped beaver and sold their hides. He was also an experienced hunter and he taught his sons hunting as well. In turn, Merle (Jim), Clarence (Gink), Roy (Dewdrop), and Cletus all became seasoned hunters, hunting deer, raccoon, opossum, ground hog, squirrel and rabbit for the family's meat. Spring and summer brought fish to the dinner table from the Little Turkey River. Once in a while they caught a big ole turtle for the soup pot, almost a delicacy.

Now Grandma Lillian, she was a feisty lady with snow white hair, forever wrapped in a bun atop her head. She regularly walked three and a half miles to town for groceries. It was never much -- a bit of flour, sugar, and Plow Boy chewing tobacco. She and Grandpa both chewed Plow Boy.

Down the hill from the cabin she kept a vegetable and flower garden, and struggled to keep the chickens out of it, as well as trying to keep the foxes away from the chickens. Chickens were an important source of meat and eggs. It gave them the protein they needed for a healthy diet.

On hot summer days Grandma slipped into her five-buckle boots, grabbed her walking stick and a five-gallon bucket; she headed off into the woods to pick blackberries, raspberries, and gooseberries. Hours passed. No one worried about her because they knew she only returned when her bucket was full. When she got back, her arms trickled with blood from scraping skin against berry bush thorns. She thought nothing of it; she grabbed a crumpled hanky from her apron pocket and wiped the blood away. The rest of her day was spent washing, plucking away bits of green, and finally preparing the berries for fresh pies and canning.

Like Grandpa, Grandma helped out with finance as best as she could. She made rabbit fur gloves, clothes from gunny sacks and flour sack aprons. She gathered honey from her bee trees; honey for eating and wax for making bees wax candles. Pure maple syrup was harvested from tapping maple trees. She prepared food, and made jams and jellies from berries. Some or maybe all of this was sold for cash, depending upon their immediate needs. Her contribution was essential to maintaining the family budget.

This wiry little old woman could do everything! I was amazed by her versatility! I always thought Grandma's life was much harder than it was for Grandpa. Grandpa's stoic, stern determination and strength led me to believe he could accomplish anything. Grandma, on the other hand, appeared more fragile. Her work was hard for a woman her size. Not only did she work hard, but she also birthed and raised nine kids. That is a job in itself. She had her hands full at all times.

Her daily chores and her children kept her BUSY, BUSY, BUSY all the time. Every morning she was up at the crack of dawn making sure the children were dressed and ready for school. She packed each of them lunch in a lard can. A bread, lard, and sugar sandwich with a piece of fruit, and they were off. On rainy days when the river raged, she made sure grandpa went to the creek to lift each child across.

Grandma mended clothes, hauled water from the creek -- which wasn't a short jaunt -- for washing clothes, and then hung them to dry. She cooked breakfast and supper every day. She canned produce and churned butter from fresh cow's milk. She loved her kids and tried to make them happy. It was a never ending round of days and nights, and not once did I hear her complain. She had chosen this life, and while Grandpa spoke few words, he expected this work from her. I thought maybe she kept her dogs, Trix and Rex, close by for love and companionship since Grandpa didn't have much to say to her.

I can't recall visiting the Old Log Cabin in winter, but I have heard my share of stories; not all so kind. Winters in the back hills could be brutal. There were times when they couldn't dig out from deep snow for days. If a visit to town was necessary, Grandpa walked to Grandma's sister Alta Bolsinger's house in Graham, Iowa; a mile and a half or so down the road. He borrowed their horse to make the trip. Sometimes even the horses barely made it through the knee-high snow. Grandpa drove them hard to cut through the drifts. On milder winter days, my older sister and her husband would make a Sunday run. She said they barreled through snow drifts up to their knees, barely making the three-quarter mile walk up from the bottom land with necessities for the grandparents.

One blustery, frigid winter night, grief settled down on the Davis family. The winds howled, cutting through the newspaper lined cabin walls and around the window sills. Snow piled up and drifted high. The cold was so pervasive the stove barely kept the cabin warm. Dorothy, the seventh child was a little over three years old and caught pneumonia. During this brutal winter night, she made a turn for the worst. The cold weakened her lungs. Grandma and Grandpa knew the doctor would not come during the storm, nor could they get her to town. She passed away that night in the arms of her oldest brother, Jim. His arms ached from trying to hold her head up, while she gasped for air. Her small, fragile frame slowly turned limp. She was gone. Her body was wrapped in cloth and placed in a pine box. She was kept deep in a hillside cave until spring, when she was laid to rest in Colesburg's Oakhill Cemetery.

Dorothy's death affected the whole family. A deep and quiet sadness fell upon them. The remaining children learned to survive the passing of their sister; after all, death was familiar to hill folks. But the oldest brother, who held her as she died, was so saddened that he swore once he left the hills, he would never return.

Years passed faster than Grandma and Grandpa expected. A son went off to the Korean War; the rest of the kids left one by one to start their lives, leaving the hills behind. Grandpa thought maybe he could find a job in a bigger city, like Dubuque, Iowa. His oldest son worked at John Deere Dubuque Works, and he was able to get grandpa work as a janitor, but factory work was not for him. He walked away several days later informing no one. He returned to the hills he loved, to his ten acres.

The kids often returned home with their children in tow to visit the grandparents and The Old Log Cabin. This pleased Grandma and Grandpa. Eventually, my mom, Mary Davis Ostrander moved back to the cabin with three small children and another on the way while my dad, Clarence E. Ostrander went away to serve in World War II. She didn't stay long. She had a taste of city life and the harsh country ways no longer appealed to her.

After my Mom moved back to Dubuque, Iowa, Grandma Lillian later became seriously ill with liver cancer. She needed a lot of medical care, and Grandpa decided that they better move to the town of Colesburg, closer to the doctors. They packed what few belongings they owned and moved. My family still made Sunday visits to see them, but visiting them in town wasn't the same as trips made to the Old Log Cabin.

After Grandma passed in 1962, Grandpa never looked back; he lost his desire to return home to his ten acres. He moved to Dubuque and joined our family, not happy with city life he went on to live with his son in Manchester. He wasn't happy there either, so he came back to our home, living with us for many years.

Eventually, his disabling age and medical needs became so great he was moved into a nursing home, dying there in August of '75. He was a man who rarely saw a doctor or took a pill. All that hard work made him tough and rarely sick throughout his life. He lived until age 88. He died from an enlarged and failing heart.

"The Old Log Cabin" and its ten acres was sold to the grandson, (Robert Ostrander) and his family in 1974.

Family Owned and Operated

Before leaving this world, Grandpa Charley sold the acreage and the weathered Old Log Cabin to my brother, Robert (Bob) Ostrander, who helped his grandparents in his younger years. He dry-walled interior walls, painted, and spread linoleum atop bare wood floors. He added a propane stove, and a battery operated refrigerator. He installed new windows. The changes made the cabin homey, and it came alive again, but not in the ways I loved the cabin from my youth. The changes took away from the way it was meant to be.

By now, I was grown up, almost sixteen; the cabin became my place of escape; I enjoyed carefree and peaceful weekends there. A few years had passed and I couldn't be there as often as I wanted because of a full time job, but I vividly remember one hot summer night. I worked second shift at Central Foam; I drove to the cabin to join in on some family fun for the weekend. My brother's wife, Sharon, was supposed to meet me at the top of the lane on her four-wheeler. In the blackness of a moonless night, I saw no glimpse of headlights. No one was there to meet me! I blew my car horn, several times, hoping someone, anyone, might hear it. **Nothing! NO ONE!** Goosebumps ran up and down my spine.

Two choices lie before me -- walk the lane or go home. After driving to get here, I wasn't going home. I had to walk that dangerous path, something I had never done alone, at midnight. I started my journey relying on matches and a cigarette lighter to light my way. I lit my lighter, but step by step, my fingers grew hotter and hotter to the touch. I threw it down in a rage of anger. A temporary but profound darkness surrounded me. I tried to strike a match. Owls screeched in the treetops. Coyotes yodeled in the distance, their sound creeping closer. I couldn't turn back! That was just as black as the path ahead. I struck another match and the flame flickered in the night breeze. My imagination kicked in ... Big Time! I was a child again, fearing the black and evil forest with its long branching arms reaching down to snatch me away.

I knew *HE* was there, watching, his slanted yellow eyes afire, his long jaws agape, thick saliva dripping to the ground. I struck another match, it lighted! Thank God! I started back down the path, knowing his attack might come at any minute. My heart raced. I lit another match and traveled another five feet. Fear choked me. But then I heard the rescuing sound of the four-wheeler! Oh Lord, thank you! Headlights! I stood in the middle of the lane, blocking out whatever danger lurked in darkness. Slowly, calm settles over me, and my thoughts told me, "I will never do this alone, again!" I could breath. I didn't want the family to know how frightened I was. They had to see for themselves just how brave I was.

Last night's horror dissolved into the sunshine of a new day. We fished and swam in the Little Turkey, rode four wheelers, mini bikes and motorcycles, and generally flitted away a bright summer day. We were kids again.

Nights were spent around the kitchen table playing dominoes or cards by candlelight or kerosene lanterns. Sometimes we told ghost stories until we scared ourselves senseless -- like the little girl chased by a bobcat until her mother saw her running to the cabin door, but ... she couldn't run fast enough! To save ourselves, we raced up the stairs to the iron squeaking beds that Grandma and Grandpa once used for their kids. We dived under the old quilts and hid ourselves until sleep saved us.

God made this hill country for solitude and reflection, and one quiet day, I wandered deep into the woods to soak up the beauty and tranquility. I was thankful for nature's abundance that had sustained my grandparents and their kids. I walked. I breathed deeply. I needed to take it all in -- the roaming hills, the beautiful valley, the bubbling spring where Grandma fetched fresh clean water; the tall, stern sentinel. The sweet fragrance of wildflowers and the tart flavor of wild berries that Grandma once picked. I can still smell and taste her homemade berry pies and her soft, delicious, fried bread that we feasted upon on those Sunday visits, a lifetime ago. The magnificent waterfall, with golden sunbeams slicing through the canopy to illuminate the water's glassy sheen. A perfect peace settles over me, a unity between woman and nature. It was magical! Everything had been here since the beginning of time.

Vickie Owens

All Great Things Must Come to an End
Lost but Never Forgotten

The Magic Disappears

All great things must end. In May of 1984, hard times fell upon my brother. He couldn't find a way to keep the Log Cabin and its ten acres. It had to be sold. A sad day for everyone. It was bought by Kahle-White LLC. They turned nine acres into forestry and the tenth acre is where the cabin remains. It is no longer the cabin I knew; it has since fallen into the sink-hole. Many Davis family members continue to visit. They walk the three quarter mile path and try to slip into the past. I imagined the Old Log Cabin that I held so dear, would always be a part of our family, but now we need permission to be on the land.

The trips dwindled. Some cousin's still get permission to hunt there, and others have had their cremated remains spread amidst the trees, fusing their souls with the forest for all time.

When I look back on my grandparents' austere way of life, I know exactly where my roots are. I know I am as frugal as they had been. I have used a wringer washer and rinse tubs to clean clothes, and to this day, I still hang laundry in fresh air to dry. I love the smell of clean clothes dried by a summer breeze and warm sunlight. I have experienced life without hot water for months at a time. I know what it is like to live in darkness lit only by candles, night after night. Yet today, a woodstove keeps the house toasty warm throughout cold winter months, and I stack the firewood for the months that lay ahead. I appreciate a beautiful garden where I eat sun-ripened tomatoes warm off the vine. I have and still live that life. I accept these ways. I do wonder from time to time if some city people could survive like this, without the conveniences of modern society. Those city conveniences may be good enough to attract me as I age. Time will tell.

The city is always awake; traffic is constant, motors roaring, loud sirens blaring, factories spewing dirt. Trains roar by, blowing loud, LOUD horns. Folks are out walking in the dead of night, and no one can guess if they are friend or foe, or if they carry a gun. Your neighbor might steal, or shoot your dog. Plastic sacks and beer cans line the highways, so now sections of road are "adopted" to be kept clean by various groups or clubs. The drinking water is processed to keep it clean. The one good thing about the city is easy access to medical care -- if one has insurance.

By comparison, the country is peaceful. I breathe clean, fresh air in the early morning, with no tall buildings blocking my view. I watch the sun rise in the East and listen to the birds sing a sweet melody. In the evening hours, I walk outside and the only things I hear are myriad frogs, croaking for a mate, noisy insects, and a few coyotes yodeling in the distance. The night is bright and clear with a gazillion stars sparkling down upon the earth and me. This aura of tranquility is nature's drug, lulling me into peace and contentment.

I don't look at any part of my life as struggle or hardship. Life might be harder, but the riches from hands-on existence are far sweeter. Everything that I have learned is a gift toward the person I have become. I am thankful for my roots and for those folks who cherish the simple life, as I do.

I am also thankful to be able to share my reflection of the hill country wisdom and insights. But best of all, I can share my wonderful Grandma Lillian's great woodstove recipes with you and the genealogy of my wonderful grandparents; where it all began from the eyes of her loving granddaughter. Grandma and Grandpa would be so pleased that I have given you a small part of their natural ways in the back hills of Colesburg, Iowa.

Grandma Lillian's Woodstove Recipes at The Old Log Cabin

Vickie Owens

SOUPS

Chicken and Dumplings

1 Stewing Chicken
1 Small Onion (chopped fine)
1 Stalk of celery chopped
Salt and pepper to taste

2 cups of flour
1 tsp of baking soda
1/2 cup of oil
1/4 cup of milk

Method: Wash and cut up chicken, put chicken
in large pot and cover with water. Boil until chicken is tender. Take out of pot let cool a bit and take chicken off the bone and set aside.

Mix flour, salt and baking powder. Mix milk and oil and add to dry ingredients. Stir until well blended and forms a dough ball with your hands. Roll out dough 1/8" thick, cut into squares and drop into boiling broth with onion and celery. Add cut up chicken. Cover and reduce heat, let cook about 30 minutes, stirring occasionally.

Great soup for a cold winter night

Homemade Dumplings

2 cups of flour
4 tsp of baking powder
1 tsp salt
2 Tbsp. of shortening
3/4 to 1 cup of milk
Broth
Method: Sift dry ingredients, add shortening
And then add milk until a thick batter is
Obtained. Drop teaspoons of batter into boiling broth. Cover and cook 3-5 minutes, be sure not to lift lid until done.

These dumplings can also be added to chicken noodle soup or potato soup.

Dumplings are also very good added to chicken and broth with some cut up celery and carrots.

Potato and Cheddar Soup

3 cups of water
3 cups of red potatoes, peeled and cubed
4 Tbsp. of butter
1 medium onion
4 Tbsp. of flour
Salt and pepper to taste
3 1/2 cups of milk
3/4 tsp of sugar
1 1/2 cups of shredded cheddar cheese
1 1/2 cups of cubed ham

Method: Bring water to boil in kettle, add potatoes, salt and pepper to taste. Cook until potatoes are tender. Drain, reserving 1 1/2 cups of liquid. May add a bit of water if needed. Melt butter in pan over medium heat, add onion, cook and stir until onion is tender. Add flour, gradually add potatoes, reserved liquid and water if needed. Add milk and sugar to onion mixture; stir well. Add ham and cheese. Simmer over low heat about 25 minutes, stirring frequently. This should make about sixteen servings. Absolutely delicious!

This soup is everyone's favorite

Hard Times Soup

6 quarts of water
2 cups of celery chopped
2 cups of onions chopped
2 cups of potatoes chopped
2 cups of summer sausage chunked
2-3 Tbsp of butter
2 eggs whipped

Method: In a large pot, bring water to boil. Add all ingredients, except the whipped eggs. Simmer for about 1 hour. Blend in the whipped eggs after 1 hour and boil for 1 minute. Let this soup chill for 8 hours or overnight. This will enhance the flavor of the soup.

This soup was made often during the
Days of the Depression

Vickie Owens

Hard Times Cabbage Soup

4 cups of cabbage, coarsely chopped
3 cups of water
1 cup of potatoes, chopped
1 sweet onion, chopped
2 Tbsp. of butter
2 slices of bacon
Salt and pepper to taste
2 Tbsp. of cornstarch
1 cup of milk

Method: This is a very simple soup. Combine the first seven ingredients and cook until tender.

Dissolve cornstarch and milk together, whip until there are no lumps, add to soup. This will thicken the soup. Wait until thickened and serve.

Cabbage is a good source of
Vitamin B2, magnesium, iron, protein, and niacin

Bean Soup

1 lb. bag of Navy Beans
8 cups of water
1 meaty ham bone
1 cup of chopped carrots
1 cup of chopped celery
3 medium potatoes peeled and diced
1/4 tsp of pepper
Dash of salt or salt to taste

Method: Let beans soak in cold water overnight. Wash them good the next day and combine beans, water, and ham bone in large pot. Bring to boil, cover and simmer for 2 hours, or until beans get tender. Add the rest of the ingredients. Cook 1 hour. Take ham bone out of soup and cut meat away from bone and add back into the soup.

Serve this soup with homemade baking powder biscuits, or with a nice warm slice of homemade bread topped with fresh butter

Vickie Owens

Winter Bean Soup

2 cups of mixed dried beans
2 quarts of water
2 cups of chopped ham
1 large onion chopped
1 large can of tomatoes chopped
2 Tbsp. of salt
1 cup of carrots chopped
1 fresh minced garlic, optional

Method: Rinse and clean beans in cold water until water runs clear. They are best if let set overnight in cold water. Place beans in a large kettle and cover with the 2 quarts of water. Simmer for 3 hours. Add onions, tomatoes, carrots, ham and garlic if you desire. Let simmer 1 hour and serve.

This sure tastes good on a cold winter day

Green Bean Soup

1 quart of green beans cut into 1" pieces
1-2 cups of carrots chopped
1-2 cups of potatoes diced
1 small onion diced
Winter celery
Salt and pepper to taste
3 Tbsp. of vinegar
1/4 tsp sugar
2 Tbsp. of flour browned
Shortening
Dash of cinnamon

Method: Combine the first 5 ingredients and cook until tender. Add vinegar, sugar, and cinnamon. Make a gravy of flour and shortening; add to soup. Sir well and this great soup is ready to be served.

Beans are best if picked straight from the garden, they have that special flavor, but canned beans will work.

Vickie Owens

Grandma's Country Lima Bean Soup

1 1/4 cups of Lima beans, rinsed and drained
1 cup of chapped ham
1/4 cup chopped onion
1/4 tsp salt
1/4 tsp black pepper
1/4 tsp of dried sage
2 cups of milk
2 Tbsp. of butter

Method: Place lima beans in your kettle, add enough water to cover the beans. Bring to a boil, reduce heat and let simmer about 5 minutes.

Remove from stove and let stand about 1 hour, covered. Drain beans and return to kettle, stir in 3 cups of water, ham, onion, salt, pepper and dried sage. Bring to boil and reduce heat to simmer for 2 1/2 to 3 hours, or until beans are tender. Add milk and butter, stir until butter is melted. This will make about eight servings.

This soup is good any time of the year

Milk Bean Soup

1 lb. of dry pea beans
Water
Milk
1 tsp salt
Bread, cubed
Butter

Method: Cook pea beans in salted water until soft. Add milk to mixture for your desired consistency. Add a little butter and salt to taste.

Use dried bread cubes placed on a cookie sheet with melted butter poured over them and toasted in the broiler. Serve toasted bread crumbs in separate bowl and add to soup if you desire.

This soup is kind of a fly by the seat of your pants kind of soup. Guess and maybe it will turn out

Tomato Soup

1 quart of tomatoes; home grown or freshly cooked
1/4 cup of onions chopped
1 tsp of salt
Pepper to taste
2 Tbsp. of butter
2 quarts of milk
1/4 tsp of baking soda

Method: Heat tomatoes, onions, salt, pepper and butter together and let simmer until blended. Add baking soda and stir. Bring mixture to a boil and reduce heat.

In the meantime, heat the milk in a large skillet that will hold all the I ingredients. Just before the milk starts to boil turn heat off and slowly pour the tomato mixture into the skillet with the milk, stirring constantly. Turn off heat and eat.

Use fresh garden tomatoes or fresh canned garden tomatoes

Vegetable Soup

1 lb. of stewing meat, browned
5-6 medium potatoes diced
1 can of corn
1 can of peas
1 can of carrots
1/2 cup of celery
Salt and pepper to taste
1 small onion diced
3 whole tomatoes diced
1 can of tomato juice
2 cups of water
1 bay leaf

Method: In kettle brown your stewing meat in butter, cover with tomato juice, and 2 cups of water, cook until meat is tender. Add the rest of ingredients and cook on low heat for about 45 minutes to 1 hour. If the soup needs more water, go ahead and add water. You may cook longer depending on your desired consistency. Take bay leaf out before eating

Be sure to use all fresh garden vegetables if you have them

Vickie Owens

Grandma's Vegetable Soup

2 cups of chicken broth
4 cups of water
2 cups of tomatoes diced
1/4 cup of celery chopped
1 cup of carrots diced
1 cup of potatoes diced
1 cup of cabbage chopped
1/2 cup okra sliced
1/2 cup of corn
1/2 cup of peas
1 garlic clove
1/4 cup of onion chopped
1 tsp salt
1 tsp pepper
1/4 tsp of chili powder
2 bay leaves

Method: Combine all ingredients in soup kettle, bring to boil and turn down heat to simmer for about an hour.

Great with baking powder biscuits

Homemade Potato Soup

5 to 6 potatoes thinly sliced
Salt and pepper to taste
1 small onion is optional

Cover potatoes with water and bring to boil until potatoes become tender.

While this is cooking, in a small bowl mix the
following: 3 eggs and flour. Enough flour to make the egg mixture crumbly.

By now the potatoes should be tender. Turn the stove down to medium heat and add your flour/egg mixture; dropping by spoonful's into the potato soup mixture, stirring often for about 10 minutes. You may add parsley flakes. If you think the potato soup is too thin you can add flour/milk mixture to the soup for thickness.

> The egg/flour droppings are also called rubs
> These rubs can be added to other soups as well

Cheesy Potato Soup

5 to 6 potatoes cubed
Salt and pepper to taste
1 medium onion chopped fine and optional
1 Tbsp. of parsley flakes
1/2 cup milk
1/2 cup butter
1 1/2 cups of cheddar cheese

Method: Combine potatoes, salt, pepper, onion, parsley flakes and cover with water; bring to boil until potatoes are tender. Turn off stove and add milk, butter and cheese, stir until cheese is melted., mixing well.

Poor Man's Stew

5 to 6 cups of water
5 to 6 medium potatoes cubed
2 large onions thinly sliced, optional
2 lbs. of hamburger
Salt and pepper to taste
5 to 6 whole cloves

Method: Cook hamburger and drain grease. Combine water, onions, salt, and pepper; bring to boil. Crumble pieces of hamburger into the mixture and bring to a boil. Add cloves and potatoes. Cover and simmer for about 20 minutes. Water will reduce 1/2 of the recipe.

When there is nothing else in the house
except potatoes, onions, hamburger and you,
this might be the day you turn to
Poor Man's Stew

Vickie Owens

Parsnip Stew

2 Tbsp. of butter
1 small onion diced
2 cups of potatoes cubed
2 cups of water
3 cups of parsnips diced
4 cups of milk
Salt and pepper to taste

Method: Cook onion in butter in a large pot over medium heat until soft. Add potatoes and water; cover and bring to boil and let cook for about 10 minutes. Add parsnips and continue to cook for about 20 minutes. Add milk and reduce heat. Season with salt and pepper. Let simmer 10 minutes, stirring occasionally.

This serves about 6 people.

> Parsnips have a taste all their own,
> somewhat starchy like a potato,
> sweet like a carrot,
> and a little nutty

Mulligan Stew

2 lbs. of ground beef or hamburger, browned
1/2 lb. pork sausage, browned
1-16 oz. can of lima beans
1-16 oz. can of red kidney beans
1 large bunch of celery diced
2 cups of carrots diced
3 cups potatoes diced
2 large onions diced
2 quarts of tomatoes crushed
Salt and pepper to taste

Method: Mix all ingredients in a large casserole dish and bake at 350 degrees F for 30-45 minutes.

Guaranteed to fill a Working Man's hunger

This dish was popular in the
early 1900's with the Hobo's

Vickie Owens

Grandma's Homemade Noodles

4 cups of flour
8 eggs
1 Tbsp. of cold water
2 tsp salt

Method: Mix all of the above ingredients, roll out on floured countertop about 1/4 inch thick. Roll up the dough and slice noodles to your thickness, shake them out and drop them in boiling chicken broth.

These noodles can also be laid out, let dry and froze for a later date. If you don't want to roll them up and cut, roll them out to ¼" and use a pizza cutter to cut them.

Chili

2 lbs. of ground beef browned
1 large can of tomatoes
1 large can of tomato sauce
2 cans of kidney beans
1 medium onion finely chopped
1/4 cup celery finely chopped
1 small green pepper finely chopped
2 Tbsp. of chili powder, or to taste
Salt and pepper to taste

Method: Brown ground beef and drain. Mix all ingredients with browned ground beef. Put in a large pot and let simmer for 1 to 1 1/2 hours. Let cool a bit and serve in bowls. Smother chili with cheese.

Chili can be put in the freezer for another meal

Vickie Owens

SALADS

Granny's German Potato Salad

1 cup of bacon cooked crispy and diced
1 1/2 cup water
2/3 cup cider vinegar
3 Tbsp. flour
1/3 cup sugar
1/2 tsp salt
1/2 tsp pepper
8 cups of cooked potatoes sliced

Method: Fry bacon crisp, keep 4 Tbsp. of bacon grease drippings in pan. Add water and vinegar; bring to a boil. Add flour, sugar, salt and pepper. Boil until thick. Pour over potatoes and bake at 350 degrees F in casserole dish until heated through, about 20-25 minutes.

This serves about 8 people.

Nothing better than nice warm potato salad
on a cold winter day

German Potato Salad

5 lbs. of red potatoes
2 tsp salt
1 tsp pepper
1 medium onion chopped fine
3/4 cup of fresh parsley chopped fine
1 1/2 Tbsp. cornstarch
3/4 cup water
3/4 cup vinegar
1/2 lb. bacon fried crispy
1 1/2 cups sugar

Method: Mix cornstarch with water. Cook and slice potatoes. Add salt, pepper, and parsley. Fry bacon crisp and crumble. Turn off fire and add vinegar and sugar. Mix well. Heat to a boil and add cornstarch mixture. Thicken slightly. Pour over potatoes, toss lightly to coat. Serve warm.

This is best made up a day ahead of time
and served warm

Vickie Owens

Asparagus Salad and Dressing

1 lb. of fresh asparagus, steamed for 5 minutes until tender and crisp
1/2 cup chopped walnuts
2 oranges peeled and sliced into sections
3 cups of lettuce chopped

Dressing

2 Tbsp. of vegetable oil
2 Tbsp. of vinegar
2 Tbsp. of orange juice
2 tsp of sugar
1/2 tsp pepper

Method: Cut cooked asparagus into 1 inch pieces, place in a bowl. Combine walnuts, orange slices, and salad greens and mix with asparagus.

In a small bowl, combine all dressing ingredients and mix well. Add the dressing to the salad and mix well. Let chill.

Serves about 4, if you wish to serve more, double the recipe.

This goes great with salmon patties or fish

Yummy to My Tummy Salad

3-3oz pkgs. of lime jello
2 cups of boiling water
1 cup sugar
1 can #303 crushed pineapple
1 cup whipping cream
1 cup of chopped walnuts
1 cup of grated cheddar cheese
2 Tbsp. of lemon juice

Method: Mix gelatin in boiling water and let cool. Add all other ingredients and chill.

Serves 8

Vickie Owens

Peach Salad

1 cup of miniature marshmallows
1 small can of crushed pineapple, drained
1 can of coconut
1 carton of sour cream
Peach halves

Method: Very simple. Mix marshmallows, pineapple, coconut and sour cream.

Serve spooned into each peach halve.

A very decorative salad

Chicken-Apple Salad

2 cups of cooked chicken, chopped
1/2 cup of coarsely chopped apple
1 cup of celery, sliced small
2 Tbsp. of raisons
1/4 cup of chopped walnuts
1/2 cup of salad dressing, your choice

Method: Mix all ingredients with your choice of salad dressing until well blended. You may garnish with shredded carrots.

Easy and fun to make salad
Make sure to keep chilled

Vickie Owens

Orange Garlic Salad

6 oranges, sliced
Garlic to taste
Salt to taste
3 to 4 Tbsp. of olive oil

Method: Peel oranges, remove pulp and slice.
Place in a mixing bowl, add garlic and salt to taste. Cover with olive oil and let stand at room temperature for about 2 hours.

Toss a bit before eating.

Cauliflower Salad

2 cups of raw cauliflower cut in small pieces
3 hardboiled eggs, chopped
1/4 cup of green onions, chopped
1/2 cup green pepper, chopped
Pepper to taste
1/3 cup of mayonnaise
5 Tbsp. of mustard
1/4 cup sunflower seeds

Method: Cook cauliflower in boiling water for about 2 minutes. Combine all the rest of the ingredients, mix well and chill.

This will serve 4-6 people

Another great salad to make and take
Great for picnics

Sweet Potato Salad

4 cups of raw, shredded sweet potatoes, about 3
1 apple, unpeeled and chopped
1/2 cup chopped walnuts
1/2 cup sour cream
1/2 cup mayonnaise
1 tsp of grated lemon rind
2 Tbsp. of lemon juice
2 Tbsp. of honey
1/2 tsp salt
1/8 tsp of pepper

Method: Combine sweet potatoes, apple and walnuts. Combine rest of ingredients in small bowl and mix well. Pour dressing over sweet potato mixture. Stir well. Cover and chill one hour.

Serves 6-8 people

This has a great taste

Old Indian Summer Salad

1 pkg. of sugar-free orange jello
3/4 cup of boiling tomato juice
1 Tbsp. of vinegar
1/2 tsp of chili powder
1/2 cup of cold tomato juice with ice
1 can of whole kernel corn
1/2 cup of celery, chopped
1/2 cup green pepper, chopped

Method: Dissolve jello in hot tomato juice, add vinegar and chili powder. Combine cold tomato juice and ice cubes to make 1 1/2 cups. Add jello mixture stirring until slightly thickened. Remove ice. Add corn, celery, and green pepper. Let stand until set. Should be ready to eat in 1 hour.

Two-Color Salad

3 envelopes of Knox Gelatin
3/4 cup of cold water
2 1/2 cups of orange juice
1 can sliced beets, drained
2/3 cup of sugar
3/4 tsp of salt
1/4 cup of mild vinegar
2 cups of celery, chopped

Method: Soften gelatin in water. Heat juice and stir in gelatin and sugar. Add salt and vinegar. Chill until syrupy. Drain beets, add 1 3/4 cups of orange juice. Pour into a 1/2-quart oiled mold. Chill until slightly firm. Add celery to the remaining orange juice mixture. Pour over beet layer. Chill until firm. Sever on lettuce.

Serves 8

Broccoli-Cauliflower Salad

2 heads of cauliflower, chunked
1 bunch of broccoli, chunked
1 red onion, chopped
1 cup of mayonnaise
1 Tbsp. of sugar
1 Tbsp. of vinegar
Salt, pepper and garlic to taste

Method: Broccoli, cauliflower and onion should be broken or cut into bite size pieces. Mix mayonnaise, sugar, vinegar, salt, pepper and garlic for the dressing. Mix all ingredients with the dressing and let chill overnight.

Serve the next day

Sauerkraut Salad

1 large can shredded sauerkraut, drained
1 cup of celery, chopped
1 cup of green pepper, chopped
1 bunch of green onions, diced
1 cup of green olives, sliced
1 1/2 cups of sugar
1/2 cup of vinegar
1 cup of vegetable oil

Method: Shake in jar the sugar, salad oil, and vinegar. Pour dressing over the rest of mixture: sauerkraut, celery, green pepper, green onion, and sliced olives. Refrigerate anywhere from 8 hours to 2 days and serve.

Serves 6-8 people

You may store this in refrigerator up to 2 weeks

Spinach Salad

4 cups of raw spinach chopped
1/4 cup of celery, chopped fine
1/4 cup onion, chopped fine
1 cup of grated sharp cheddar cheese
6 large boiled eggs, chopped
1/2 tsp of salt

Dressing: 1 Tbsp. of white vinegar or lemon juice, 3 Tbsp. of mayonnaise, and 1/2 tsp of salt. Whip.

Method: Mix salad ingredients, add dressing and fold lightly.

                    Ready to serve

Spinach lovers will be sure to enjoy this salad
Use your spinach fresh out of the garden

Country Corned Beef Salad

1 1/2 lbs. of roasted beef, cut into thin strips
1 red bell pepper, diced
1 green bell pepper, diced
2 cups of sweet corn, thawed
4 cups of new red potatoes, cooked and cubed
4 green onions, sliced thin
3 green chilies, minced

Dressing: 1 1/2 cups mayonnaise, 1/2 cup olive oil, 1/2 cup balsamic vinegar, 2 Tbsp. of sugar, 2 tsp of salt, 2 tsp of fresh pepper.

Combine all dressing ingredients and whisk until thoroughly blended.

Method: Roast a tender 2 lb. beef roast at 325 degrees F until tender; cool roast and remove all fat. Cut into very thin strips. Combine beef with all other ingredients for salad. Fold dressing into mixture and serve at room temperature.

A nice hearty salad

Coleslaw

1 medium head of cabbage, shredded
1 small onion, chopped
1 green pepper, chopped
3 carrots, grated

Dressing:
1/2 cup of corn oil
1 cup vinegar
1/2 tsp celery seed
1 tsp mustard
3/4 cup sugar
Boil sugar, vinegar, oil and seasoning together. Let cool.

Method: Pour dressing over vegetable mixture, mix well and let chill in refrigerator for at least 24 hours.

Coleslaw is great with fish dinner

Deviled Eggs

6 eggs, hard boiled, cooled and slice in half
Salt and pepper to taste
Mayonnaise or Miracle Whip
1/2 tsp of vinegar, optional
Paprika

Method. Cut eggs to halve lengthwise. Remove yolks, mash, and moisten with mayonnaise and vinegar mixture, salt and pepper until creamy. Lightly scoop mixture into each empty egg halve. Top each egg with a sprinkle of paprika.

Deviled eggs are great for all occasions
You may also sprinkle them with crumbled bacon or cheese

Carrot Raison Salad

4 Cups of shredded carrots
1 Cup of raisons
1/2 tsp salt
1/2 cup mayonnaise
1/2 cup sour cream
1 Tbsp. of brown sugar

Method: Mix carrots and raisons together. Then mix the sour cream, mayonnaise, brown sugar and salt altogether. Add carrots and raisons to this mixture and make sure carrots are well coated. Refrigerate for 1 hour and serve cold.

You may also add walnuts for extra flavor.

Cut up dates may be substituted for raisons

Vickie Owens

BREADS, BISCUITS & PANCAKES

Vickie Owens

Hard Times Bread

1 cup of flour
1 tsp baking powder
Water

Method: Stir in enough water to make a batter, pour into greased skillet. This is best in a cast iron skillet. Fry until golden brown on each side, like a pancake

For those of you who did not live through the great depression, this bread was used often to satisfy their needs.

Try it, you might like it

Date and Nut Bread

1 tsp baking soda
3/4 cup of hot water
1 cup of dates, pitted and cut up fine
1 large Tbsp. of butter
1 egg, beaten
3/4 cup of sugar
3/4 cup walnuts, chopped
1/4 tsp salt
1 1/2 cups of flour

Method: Mix baking soda and hot water and pour of over dates. Add remaining ingredients and mix altogether. Pour in lightly greased loaf pan. Bake at 325 F for 1 hour.

Let stand 10 minutes in baking pan, take out and let cool.

Cut and serve

Vickie Owens

Black Walnut Bread

3 cups of all-purpose flour, sifted
4 1/2 tsp baking powder
1/2 cup sugar
1 tsp salt
1 cup of chopped black walnuts
2 eggs
1 cup of milk
1/4 cup of butter, melted

Method: Sift flour, baking powder, sugar and salt together. Add black walnuts. Beat eggs, milk and melted butter. Add flour mixture and stir until thoroughly blended. Don't attempt to beat all the lumps. Spoon inside a greased loaf pan and bake in a 350-degree F oven that has been pre-heated, bake for 1 hour. Turn out of pan and cool before serving.

This is also very good served slightly warm
with butter and honey

Grandma's Applesauce Bread

1/2 cup of white sugar
1/2 cup of brown sugar
1 cup of applesauce
1 tsp of vanilla
1 tsp baking soda
1/2 tsp of cinnamon
1/2 tsp of nutmeg
1/2 tsp of pumpkin pie spice
1/2 cup of butter
2 eggs
1/3 cup of milk
2 cups of all-purpose flour
1/2 tsp salt

Method: Heat oven to 350-degree F. Grease bottom only of bread pan. In a very large bowl mix all ingredients well. Pour into baking pan and bake 60-65 minutes or until toothpick inserted in the center comes out clean. Cool about 5 minutes and remove from pan. Finish cooling on wire rack. When cool wrap in plastic wrap and store in ice box.

This makes one delicious loaf to be enjoyed

Oatmeal Bread

3/4 cup of milk
1 package of active dry yeast, or 1 cake of yeast compressed
1 cup of quick cooking oats, oatmeal
1 1/4 cups of boiling water
1 1/2 tsp of salt
1/2 cup of dry molasses
1 Tbsp. of butter
5 cups of all-purpose flour,

Method: Heat milk until a film forms. Skim surface of milk. Remove from heat when lukewarm and stir in yeast. Put oatmeal in a large bowl and stir in boiling water, salt, molasses, and butter. Cool to lukewarm. Mix in flour and milk thoroughly. Use hands because this dough is very heavy. Cover with tea towel and sit in warm area away from drafts until dough rises twice its size; about 1 1/2 hours. Turn on a floured board and knead lightly about 3 minutes. Divide in half, form into loaves and place in greased loaf pans. Let bread rise in loaf pans, double its size. Bake in 350-degree F preheated oven for about 1 hour. Remove from oven and brush tops of loaves with butter. Cool slightly and remove from pans. Let cool completely on wire rack. This bread is delicious and keeps well.

Grandma's Salt Rising Bread

2 cups of milk
2 cups of white corn meal
1 Tbsp. of sugar
1 tsp of salt
1/2 tsp baking soda
8-10 cups of all-purpose flour
2 Tbsp. of shortening
1 cup of warm water

Method: Scald milk, remove from heat, stir in corn meal, sugar and salt until smooth. Cover with a tea towel and set in a warm place overnight.
The following morning add 1 cup of warm water, mixed with baking soda and about 2 1/2 cups of flour, (enough flour to make stiff batter). Set this bowl of batter in warm water, cover and let stand until it foams up, (2 hours to a half day). Try to keep the water at an even temperature, not too hot or not too cold. If it seems the batter is not rising give it a stir to help it along. When the batter has risen knead in more shortening and more flour. It may take as many as 6-8 cups of flour to make a stiff bread dough. Shape into two loaves, and place in greased loaf pans and let rise until double in size. Bake at 350 degrees F for about 1 hour or until top of bread is golden. Wipe butter over top when taken out of oven and let cool on wire rack.

White Bread

1 cake yeast
1 1/2 quarts of warm water milk, (105-115 degree)
16 cups of white flour, if more flour is needed, add
1 egg
2 Tbsp. of sugar
2 Tbsp. of lard, melted
Butter

Method: Dissolve yeast and sugar in 1 quart of warm milk, (2% or whole milk). Add 6 cups of flour and beat well. Cover with tea towel and let rise in warm place for about 1 1/2 hours. Add rest of ingredients, and knead thoroughly. Place in greased bowl and let rise 2 more hours. Mold into 4 loaves and place in greased bread pans, cover with tea towel and let rise one more hour. Bake 10 minutes in 350-degree F pre-heated oven, and then 30-35 minutes at 300-degree F. Take out, butter the tops of your loaves and let cool on wire rack.

These loaves can be wrapped in foil and frozen

Raison Bread

3 cups of flour
1 tsp salt
3 tsp of baking powder
1 1/2 tsp of sugar
1 cup of raisons
1 1/2 cups of milk
2 Tbsp. of butter
1 egg, beaten

Method: In a large bowl combine flour, salt, baking powder, and sugar. Mix thoroughly. Add remaining ingredients and mix well. Pour into a greased loaf pan and bake at 350-degree F for about 50 minutes or until inserted toothpick in center comes out clean. Remove from pan and let cool on wire rack.

Very good when drizzled with white frosted glaze over the top of the loaf and let harden

Vickie Owens

Corn Bread

1 1/2 cups of yellow corn meal
1/2 cup of wheat flour
1/4 cup of brown sugar
1/2 tsp of baking soda
1 tsp of salt
1 cup of raisons
1 egg
1 1/4 cups of sour cream
1 cup of milk
1/4 cup butter, melted

Method: Mix together corn meal, flour, sugar, baking soda, salt and raisons. Place a tablespoon of butter in a heavy skillet, (preferably cast iron) and put in the oven. In another bowl, beat together the egg, sour cream, milk and butter. Add to your first mixture and stir well. Pour into the hot skillet and bake at 400 degrees F for 30 minutes.

Test with toothpick for doneness.

This was said to be the best darn cornbread in
The Hill Country

Grandma's Reliable Corn Bread

1 cup of yellow corn meal
1 cup of all-purpose flour
2 Tbsp. of baking powder
1 tsp of salt
1/3 cup of shortening, softened
1 cup of milk
1 egg
1/2 to 1 cup of sugar, optional

Method: Stir dry ingredient in mixing bowl. Cut in shortening until well blended. Beat milk and egg together. Mix with dry ingredients until just blended. If desired add 1/2 to 1 cup of sugar to sweeten. Mix well. Pour into a well-greased 8" pan and bake at 400 degrees F for 25 minutes.

Corn bread is always best warm out of the oven
and smothered with butter

Vickie Owens

Cream Biscuits

2 cups of all-purpose flour
1/2 tsp of salt
3 tsp of baking powder
1 cup of heavy cream

Method: Sift flour, salt and baking powder in a bowl. In a second bowl, whop cream until stiff enough to hold shape. Combine cream and flour mixture with a fork. Put flour mixture on a lightly floured board and knead about 1 minute. Pat dough 1/2" thick and cut with a biscuit cutter or kitchen glass. Bake in pre-heated oven at 450 degrees F for about 12 minutes. Serve hot with melted butter or honey.

This recipe makes about 12 biscuits

Very easy and quick biscuit to make

Buttermilk Biscuits

2 cups of self-rising flour
1 tsp of salt
1/4 cup of buttermilk
1/4 cup of water
1/4 cup of mayonnaise
Butter, melted

Method: Mix all ingredients together. Stir into small ball. Place dough on a floured board and knead lightly. Roll out dough on floured board about 1/2" in thickness. Cut with biscuit cutter or kitchen glass. Place on baking sheet and bake at 450-degree F for about 10 minutes or until golden brown. Take out of oven and brush with melted butter. Eat while still warm; this is when they are best.

A very good biscuit to go with breakfast, or any meal

Buttermilk Biscuits

1/2 cup of sesame seeds
2 cups of sifted all-purpose flour
1/2 tsp of salt
1 tsp of baking powder
1/2 cup of shortening
1/4 cup of milk
Coarse salt

Method: While you make the dough toast sesame seeds in a shallow pan in a 350-degree F oven.

Sift together flour, salt and baking powder. Cream shortening until soft and add flour mixture, working it with your hands until well combined. Next, work in baked seeds. Gradually add milk, stirring with a fork until dough holds together and has the feel of pastry. Roll paper thin on a lightly floured board and cut with a very small biscuit cutter. Place on a cookie sheet and bake at 350-degree F for 10-12 minutes. Sprinkle with coarse salt while the biscuits are still hot.

Squash Donuts

1 cup of milk
1 cup of cooked squash
1/2 tsp of salt
12 tsp of cinnamon
1/2 tsp of nutmeg
3 cups of flour
1 1/4 cups of sugar
2 Tbsp. of shortening
3 eggs, well beaten
1 tsp of vanilla

Method: Cream shortening and sugar. Add eggs, squash and vanilla. Sift flour, salt, baking powder, and spices. Add alternately with milk to shortening and sugar mixture. Chill dough. Once chilled turn onto a floured board and roll out about 1/4" thick. Cut with floured donut cutter. Fry in deep fat fryer or iron skillet with oil at about 350-degree F until golden brown. Drain on crumpled absorbing paper.
You may sprinkle with powdered sugar or white sugar while still hot.

This makes a wonderful breakfast treat

Vickie Owens

Cheese Potato Cakes

2 cups of well-seasoned mashed potatoes
1/2 cup of grated cheddar cheese
Salt and pepper to taste

Method: Combine potatoes and cheese. Form into cakes and fry in small amount of hot fat. Season as you desire.

These cheese potato cakes make a great breakfast meal with eggs and bacon

Don't throw out your leftover mashed potatoes. Keep them for a quick an easy next meal

Buttermilk Pancakes

1 1/2 cups of all-purpose flour
1/2 tsp of baking powder
1/4 tsp of salt
1/2 Tbsp. of sugar
1 egg
1 1/4 cups of buttermilk
2 Tbsp. of melted butter

Method: Sift together flour, sugar, salt and baking powder. Beat egg vigorously and stir in buttermilk and butter. Combing with flour mixture, using as few strokes as possible; over beating will toughen the pancakes. Mixture will be lumpy. Drop batter by spoonsful onto a hot greased griddle. When large bubbles appear and begin to burst it is time to turn the pancake over and brown the other side.

Serve at once while hot.

Butter and fresh maple syrup make these divine
Honey or jelly can be used as well

Vickie Owens

Potato Pancakes

2 eggs
2 cups of grated potatoes
1 1/2 tsp of salt
1 Tbsp. of flour
A pinch of baking powder

Method: Beat eggs and mix with other ingredients. Drop batter on well-greased griddle. Spider the batter. Brown on both sides and serve with homemade apple sauce.

Quick and Easy

Buckwheat Pancakes

1/2 pkg. of dry yeast
1/2 cake yeast compressed
1/4 cup of lukewarm water
2 cups of milk
2 cups of buckwheat flour
1/2 tsp of salt
1 Tbsp. of molasses
1 scant tsp of baking soda

Method: Dissolve yeast in lukewarm water. Scald milk; cool to lukewarm. Blend together yeast, milk, buckwheat flour, and salt; beating hard for 2 minutes. Cover with tea towel and let stand at room temperature overnight. Next day: mix in molasses, baking soda and 1/4 cup warm water. Pour onto a greased, hot griddle. Brown on both sides and serve piping hot.

Cover with butter and warm maple syrup

Creamed Waffles

1 cup of sifted all-purpose flour
4 tsp of baking powder
1/4 tsp of salt
3 eggs, separated
1 cup of heavy cream

Method: Sift together flour, baking powder and salt, set aside. Beat egg yolks vigorously and then add the heavy cream and continue beating hard. Stir in flour mixture and beat with a rotary beater until smooth. Beat egg whites until stiff and fold egg whites into mixture. Refrigerate 1/2 hour. Bake in pre-heated waffle iron until crisp and a delicate brown.

Serve with butter and warm honey or maple syrup.

The number of waffles depends on
the size of your waffle iron

Quick Pizza Dough

2 cups of flour
1 tsp of salt
4 tsp of baking powder
1/3 cup of oil
1/4 cup of milk

Method: Mix all dry ingredients. Add oil and milk. Stir with a fork, shape into a ball and let dough sit for a few minutes and roll out on floured board, the size crust you need.

Top crust with pizza sauce and all your favorite toppings and cover with cheese of your choice. Bake at 350-degree F for about 15-25 minutes.

Absolutely delicious

MEATS & WILD GAME

Vickie Owens

Grandma's Oven Fried Chicken

2-2 1/2 lb. frying chicken
Sweet skim milk
2 cups of dry bread crumbs, rolled fine
2 tsp of salt
2 tsp of paprika
1 tsp of lemon pepper
1/2 tsp of thyme
1/2 tsp of tarragon
1/2 tsp parsley
1/2 tsp sage
1/3 cup of cooking oil

Method: Cut chicken into serving pieces. Place in shallow baking pan and completely cover with milk. Let stand 1 hour. In a bowl combine bread crumbs, salt, paprika, lemon pepper, thyme, tarragon, parsley, and sage. Take chicken out of milk after soaking, roll in dry ingredients and place in baking pan with the 1/3 cup oil and bake at 350 degrees F for one hour.

Finger licking good

Fried and Roasted Chicken

1/3 to 1/2 cup of flour
1/2 tsp of salt
1/2 tsp of pepper
2eggs, lightly beaten
2 cups of oil or shortening
2 1/2-3 lb. frying chicken, cut into pieces

Method: Combine first three ingredients and put in a plastic bag and shake. Next, dip chicken in eggs, put in plastic bag and cover well with dry ingredients. Do each piece of chicken like this. Heat oil in large skillet. Add chicken to hot oil and brown over medium heat on all sides. Remove from skillet and place in roasting pan. Bake at 350-degree F for 45 to 60 minutes.

Serves about 4-6 people

Everyone will love this fried, roasted chicken

Vickie Owens

Country Cabin Chicken

1 cut up chicken
4-5 slices of bacon
1/2 medium onion
Celery leaves
Flour for rolling chicken

Method: Salt chicken and roll each piece in flour until coated. Place in a roasting pan. Lay slices of raw bacon on each piece of chicken. Cover chicken with water, dice onion and put in roasting pot with chicken and bake at 350 degrees F for about 2 1/2 –3 hours.

Goes well with potato salad and baked beans,
which can be made ahead of time

Country Cola Chicken

1 chicken cut up
1/2 cup ketchup
1 can of coke

Method: Mix coke and ketchup together. Put chicken in a 9x13 baking pan and pour ketchup/coke mixture over chicken. Bake at 400-degree F for 1 hour.

This recipe doesn't come much easier or tastier
Go about your business; dinner will be ready in no time

Vickie Owens

Baked Pheasant

1/3 cup of lemon juice
1/4 cup of salad oil
1/4 clove of garlic, minced
1 medium onion, minced
1 tsp salt
1/4 tsp pepper
1/8 tsp Worcestershire sauce

Method: Mix all ingredients together. Cut up pheasant and marinate in mixture over-night, turn occasionally. Drain. Flour pheasant, and brown in hot oil in skillet. Put in roasting pan, and bake at 350-degree F oven for 1 hour.

There will be enough marinate for three pheasants
This can also be cooked over a hot open fire

Chicken and Dumplings

1 chicken boiled, water just covering the chicken and season with celery, salt and pepper to taste. Boil about 30 minutes or until chicken is tender. Take whole chicken out, let cool, take meat off bone and cut up in small pieces.

Dumplings

1 cup of all-purpose flour
A pinch of salt
1 Tbsp. of cooking oil
Enough water to make a dough mixture

Roll out mixture and cut into squares

Return cut up chicken to broth, drop dumplings in one by one into boiling chicken broth and cook about 10-15 minutes.

Some like to add sliced carrots to the broth

Plain Swiss Steak

1 lb. of chuck steak cut 1" thick
1 tsp of salt
1 cup of boiling water
1/3 cup of cooking fat
Flour
1 cup of sour cream

Method: Rub meat with salt, pound flour into steak. Sear in hot fat, add water and cover. Simmer slowly until meat is tender. You may substitute 1 cup of tomatoes for the water. Add 1 cup of sour cream about 30 minutes prior to the meat being done.

This serves about 4 people

Round Steak

1 sirloin steak cut 2" thick
2 Tbsp. of butter
Salt and pepper to taste
1 small onion
Flour
1/4 cup cooking oil

Method: Season steak with salt and pepper, roll in flour and put in hot oiled pan on medium heat. Cover with onions and butter. Cook until browned on both sides, add water as you go and let simmer for about an hour.

Remaining juices from steak make an excellent gravy

Vickie Owens

Broiled Steak

1 Sirloin or Porterhouse steak
In hot cast iron skillet fry steak, smothered in salt, pepper, garlic salt, and sliced sweet onion until meat gets puffy and well browned on both sides. Turn frequently

About 3 minutes on each side; longer if you want it well done.

Modern Day: put in oven broiler, 3 minutes on each side, or longer if you want it well done.

You can use any of your favorite seasonings, but we used what was available at the cabin.

.

Great with a garden fresh salad
Corn on the cob
Fresh garden tomatoes
Toasted homemade bread

Pot Roast

3 lbs. of Rump, Chuck or Shoulder roast
3 cups of water
1 large onion
Salt and pepper to taste

Method: Put roast in roasting pan, salt and pepper to taste. Slice large onion and place over the roast. Pour 3 cups of water in roasting pan. Cover and bake at 350-degree F for approximately 3 hours. Check water level on roast every hour and add as needed. This water and juices from roast will be for your gravy.

One hour before roast is done, cube potatoes and put in roaster with roast, along with fresh carrots out of the garden and let cook for the last hour.

Gravy: Mix cornstarch and milk or water to a nice thick consistency. When roast is done remove roast, potatoes and carrots from pan and bring juices to a boil on top of the stove, add cornstarch mixture to boiling juices whisking continually until you get the thickness of the gravy just right.

Meal complete in one roaster pan
May add other seasons of your choice

Vickie Owens

Roast Beef

1-3lb Chuck roast
1 large onion, sliced
1-2 lb. bag of potatoes, cubed
Sat and pepper to taste
1 Tbsp. of garlic salt
2-3 cups of water

Method: Place roast in roasting pan, smother with sliced onions, salt, pepper and garlic salt. Add about 2 cups of water to cover bottom of roasting pan, roast at 350-degree F for 2 hours.

Add carrots and potatoes after 2 hours and let roast another hour. Three hours' total.

Use beef drippings for your gravy.

Mix left over beef, carrots and potatoes all together add to gravy and warm the next day for lunch; eating over bread

Baked Ham

1 Shoulder ham
2 cups of bread crumbs
2 Tbsp. of molasses
2 Tbsp. of melted butter
Cloves
2 Tbsp. of brown sugar
2 tsp of yellow mustard
Vinegar and sugar to taste

Method: Wash ham, place in a large kettle, cover with water. To each quart of water added, add 1/4 cup of sugar and 2 Tbsp. of vinegar. Place over slow fire, heat slowly to boiling, simmer until tender. Let ham remain in broth until cold. Skin ham, stick cloves in fat at 1" intervals. Combine bread crumbs, sugar, molasses, mustard and butter. Spread on ham. Bake at 350-degree F oven. Baste with ham broth for about an hour.

The taste of this ham is fabulous

Vickie Owens

Fresh Pork Chops

1 pkg. pork chops or fresh pork chops
Salt and pepper
1 can of Golden Mushroom soup

Method: Season pork chops with salt and pepper and fry in hot oil until brown on both sides. About 15 minutes. Remove from stove and put in baking dish. Spread one can of Golden Mushroom soup over the top of pork chops, cover with foil and bake at 350-degree F for about 45 minutes.

Very tender and delicious

Sweet and Sour Spare Ribs

3 lbs. of pork spare ribs
1/2 cup of soy sauce
1 cup of water
1 Tbsp. of salt
1 inch of ginger root
1/2 cup of brown sugar
1/2 cup of flour
3/4 cup of vinegar
1 clove of garlic
Dash of spice

Method: Cut spare ribs into 2x2" pieces. Soak them in flour and soy sauce for about 30 minutes. Brown in cooking oil. Add the rest of ingredients and simmer for 50 minutes or until tender. Serve with pineapple.

Great served with rice on the side

Meat Loaf

1 lb. of ground beef
2 Tbsp. of melted butter
1 egg, slightly beaten
2 Tbsp. of chopped onion
1 cup of coarsely broken crackers
1 cup of milk
1 tsp of salt
2 slices of bacon
Ketchup

Method: Combine all ingredients except bacon and ketchup. Form into a loaf and place in a baking pan, lay bacon across the top of the meatloaf. Bake at 350-degree F for 1 1/2 hours. Top with ketchup after an hour of baking.

Meatloaf is great with a baked potato
and vegetable of your choice

Sloppy Vegetable Burgers

1 lb. of hamburger
1 can of vegetable beef soup

Method: Fry, crumble and drain hamburger. Add 1 can of vegetable soup. Mix together and serve on a hamburger bun with ketchup, mustard and mozzarella cheese.

This is a great, fast easy meal.

Great for picnics or a fast easy meal
Eat with fries or chips

Vickie Owens

Grilled Dove

Dove, 2 birds per person
Salt
Pepper
Worcestershire sauce
1 slice of bacon per bird

Method: Sprinkle dove with salt, pepper, and Worcestershire sauce. Wrap each dove with a slice of bacon. Cook over medium open fire for about 30 minutes or until done. Turn dove over fire as needed.

Can you imagine eating something as beautiful as Dove?

A delicacy eaten over open camp fire with grilled bell peppers and cherry tomatoes

Roasted Duck with Oyster Dressing

1 medium duck

Dressing

1 tsp of salt
1/4 tsp of pepper
1 quart of bread stuffing
1 cup oysters
1/4 cup of butter
1/4 cup of lemon juice
1/4 tsp of paprika
1/8 tsp of thyme

Method: Season duck with salt and pepper. Place duck in roasting pan. Add oysters, (drained and chopped) to bread stuffing. Reserve the oyster juice for the stuffing. Put stuffing all around the duck in roasting pan. Mix butter, lemon juice, paprika, and thyme. Bake at 350 degrees F in oven for about 2 1/2 hours. Baste with lemon juice mixture often. Bake at least 1/4 of time uncovered.

Perfect Sunday dinner

Baked Coon

1 nice fat coon cleaned well and cut up
2 onions, sliced
6 cloves of garlic, chopped
Salt and pepper to taste

Method: Boil coon until very tender. Remove coon from boiling water and put in roasting pan with enough water to cover bottom of pan. Salt and pepper to taste, add onions and cloves and bake at 350-degree F for 1 hour.

This is very good served with buttered yams and green beans

Coon is an animal of many uses: it is hunted for sportsmanship
Eaten for its good taste and its hides were sold for
family income

Roast Rabbit

Dress rabbit, this does not mean in clothes!

Wash rabbit carefully in water and to each quart of water add 1/2 tsp of baking soda. When rabbit is clean let stand overnight in cold salt water.

Stuff rabbit with onion and celery. Sew up. Rub rabbit with bay leaf. Add 1 diced carrot and a few peppercorns. Dot with cooking fat. Sift a little flour over the top of the rabbit. Pour 1 cup of stock or water in the roasting pan, cover tightly. Roast in moderate oven at 400-degree F until tender. Baste with juices frequently.

Serve with slices of lemon and cranberry or Current jelly

Enjoy a cute little bunny for dinner

Vickie Owens

Fried Rabbit

2 dressed rabbits

Wash thoroughly in salt water and cut into pieces for serving. Soak overnight in salt water

Par boil in salt water until tender. A small diced onion may be added for extra flavor while parboiling.

Drain and save broth

Roll cut up pieces of parboiled rabbit in flour, brown in hot butter or fat until tender and golden brown.

You can make a sauce by adding flour or cornstarch to the broth and a touch of vinegar

Drizzle sauce over fried rabbit

Fried Squirrel

Choose as many squirrel needed per family size. For a medium size family, about 6 squirrels

Wash thoroughly in salt water and cut into pieces for serving. Soak overnight in salt water and drain.

If necessary, par boil in salt water until tender.

Roll in flour, season with salt and pepper, fry in cooking oil or fat until tender and brown.

Serve squirrel with lemon slices and parsley

Brown sauce can also be used for gravy

Squirrel Stew

6 squirrel, cleaned and soaked in salt water
3 tsp of salt
3 chicken bouillon cubes
1 tsp pepper
1 1/2 cup of celery, chopped
1 1/2 cups of onion, chopped
1 cup of green pepper, chopped
1 Quart tomatoes, cut up
1 can of cream style corn
4 medium potatoes cook and cubed
Red pepper to taste
Sugar to taste

Method: Cook cut up squirrels, salt, pepper, and bouillon cubes in pressure cooker for about 30 minutes or until tender. Cool and remove squirrel meat from bones. Add potatoes, tomatoes, corn, onion, celery, green pepper, red pepper, and sugar to squirrel broth. Simmer on low heat until thick. Add squirrel meat just before serving and give a good stir.

Beer Battered Fish

6 of any kind of your favorite fish, staked out
2 cups of beer
2 cups of flour
1 tsp of salt
1 tsp of pepper
1 cup of vegetable oil

Method: Clean and pat fish dry. Mix beer, flour, salt, pepper and vegetable oil in a bowl making a nice thick batter.

Dip each fish in batter and put in a hot greased iron skillet. Fry on each side until golden brown.

You may drip fresh lemon juice over fish before eating

Catfish tends to be the best with this
Beer Batter Recipe

Baked Trout

4 whole filleted trout
1 lemon cut up in 8 wedges
4 strips of bacon, halved
1 whole onion cut in 8 pieces
1 tsp of butter
Salt to taste

Method: Preheat oven to 400-degree F. Rub cavity of each trout with butter and salt. Place 2 wedges of onion and 2 wedges of lemon in each cavity of trout.

Lay out foil to wrap trout. Lay trout on foil with a piece of bacon on the bottom and a piece of bacon on the top. Wrap tightly and place in 400-degree F oven for about 30 minutes

Serve while hot

Great served with coleslaw and sliced tomatoes
fresh out of the garden with a nice slice of
homemade bread on the side

Fresh Trout with Stuffing

Trout whole and dressed
3 Tbsp. of butter
1/4 cup of water
1 tsp of salt
4 cups of dried bread crumbs
1/2 lb of mushrooms, sliced
1 small onion

Method: Cook onion, butter and water until onion is soft and pour over bread crumbs. Mix slightly.

Add mushrooms, salt and pepper to taste. Fill the fish cavity with dressing. Wrap fish in foil. Bake at 375-degree F for 20-25 minutes

Vickie Owens

Venison Chili

1 lb. of ground venison
1 cup of onion chopped
1 lb. of tomatoes, cut in chunks
1 can of kidney beans
1 green pepper, chopped small
8 oz. of tomato sauce
1 tsp of salt
2 tsp of chili powder
1 tsp of garlic

Method: In heavy skillet fry venison and onion until browned and tender. Drain. In kettle add venison meat, onion, tomatoes, kidney beans, green pepper, tomato sauce, salt, chili powder and garlic. Cover and simmer for 1 to 1 1/2 hours.

Serve with shredded cheese on top,
or maybe some soda crackers to go with it

Venison is good cooked in several different ways; burgers, steaks, sausage, jerky or in casseroles

Salmon Loaf

1 cup of salmon
1/4 cup of oil
2 eggs
1/2 cup of milk
12 crackers

Method: Crush crackers very fine. Mix all ingredients together and bake in a lightly greased loaf pan at 350-degree F for 45 minutes to 1 hour.

You can also make salmon patties out of this same mixture. Form into patties and fry in a little hot oil or butter until golden brown on each side.

There is no need to take the bones out of salmon,
they are very soft and edible

Salmon is always good served with fried potatoes and cream style corn and a bit of cottage cheese

Vickie Owens

Opossum

1 Big fat possum

Once you get the possum skinned, cleaned and cut up in pieces add it to a kettle of salt water and let it set for about 4 hours to get tender.

Take it out of the salt water and add it to a fresh pot of water with 2 heaping Tbsp. of butter, salt, pepper, thyme and a big spoon of sugar to sweeten it up a bit. Let it cook with the lid on. Check it about every 15 minutes to make sure it is not boiling down, if need to, add more water. Keep putting the juice over top the possum to keep it moist.

Let cook about 2 hours or until meat falls off the bone. Serve up with some boiled potatoes and vegetable of your choice.

Uncle Clete always said,
"Anything that ran across the yard at the cabin
was another meal on the table!"

The Delicacy of the Evening Turtle

Make sure your turtle is cleaned and meat of turtle is cut up in pieces. Let set in salt water for a few hours.

Next take your turtle meat and soak in milk, add your favorite seasoning to the milk and make sure the milk covers the turtle. While turtle is soaking make your batter.

Batter
2 cups of flour
Salt to taste
Pepper to taste
2 Tbsp. of garlic
2 Tbsp. of onion powder
2 Tbsp. of paprika
Mix well. Turtle should be done soaking in milk, about 15 minutes

Coat turtle in flour batter and fry in hot grease in the old iron skillet until golden brown on all sides.

CASSEROLES

Vickie Owens

Sausage and Kraut Bake

6 fully cooked polish sausage
1/4 cup of brown sugar, packed
1 jar, 32 oz. Sauer Kraut, lightly drained
1/2 cup of green pepper, finely chopped
1/2 cup of shredded Swiss cheese

Method: Cook sausage fully on top of the stove until brown. Mix kraut, brown sugar, green pepper and cook on top of stove until hot through.

Put kraut mixture in baking dish, cover with sausage and sprinkle with 1/2 cup of shredded Swiss cheese. Bake at 350-degree F for about 10 minutes, until cheese is fully melted.

Serves about 6 people

A great quick casserole if you like kraut

Sausage and Bread Bake

8 slices of white bread
2 cups of shredded cheddar cheese
1 lb. of pork sausage links
6 eggs
2 3/4 cups of milk
1/4 tsp of butter
1/4 tsp of garlic salt

Method: Lay bread on the bottom of a 9X12" greased baking dish. Sprinkle cheddar cheese over the bread. Cut up sausages in small chunks and spread over top of cheese.

Beat eggs, milk, butter and garlic salt in a bowl. Pour this mixture over the bread, sausage cheese in the baking dish. Cover and refrigerate 4-6 hours.

Preheat oven to 325-degree F. Bake about 1 1/2 hours, until brown.

Makes about 6 servings

A beautiful morning breakfast to wake up to

Vickie Owens

Egg and Sausage Casserole

1/2 lb. of pork sausage, fresh is best
3 Tbsp. of butter
2 Tbsp. of all-purpose flour
1/4 tsp of pepper
1/4 tsp of salt
1 1/4 cups of milk
2 1/2 cups of shredded fresh potatoes
3 eggs, hard boiled and sliced
1/4 cup of onion, sliced thin
1/4 cup of corn flake crumbs

Method: Preheat oven to 350-degree F. Grease an oval baking dish or 9x12 cake pan. Crumble sausage in skillet and fry until pink is gone. Drain grease from sausage. Melt 2 Tbsp. of butter in skillet over medium heat. Stir in flour, salt and pepper until smooth. Gradually add milk stirring constantly until thick and smooth. Add sausage, potatoes, eggs and onions. Stir to combine all ingredients. Add corn flakes and stir. Pour into greased baking dish or pan and bake 35-40 minutes or until potatoes are done.

Makes 6-8 servings.

Countryside Casserole

6 slices of white bread, torn into pieces
1 1/4 cups of milk
3 eggs
1/2 tsp of garlic powder
1/2 tsp of paprika
1 cup of cubed ham
2 1/2 cups of shredded cheddar cheese
1/2 cup of onion, chopped

Method: Heat oven to 375 degrees F. In large mixing bowl combine torn bread, milk, eggs, garlic powder, and paprika. Beat until smooth. Stir in ham chunks and 1 cup of cheddar cheese. Pour into a well-greased 9x12" baking pan. Bake for 25 minutes. Pull out of oven and add rest of cheddar cheese to the top and bake about 5 more minutes until the cheese is melted on top of casserole.

Let stand a few minutes before serving

.

Another great hill country breakfast

Vickie Owens

Lima Bean Casserole

2 cups of cooked dried Lima Beans
1/2 cup of sweet and condensed milk
1/2 cup of water
2 eggs, well beaten
2 Tbsp. of onion, chopped
1 tsp of salt
1/2 tsp of paprika

Method: Combine all ingredients and pour into a well-greased baking dish. Bake in a preheated 350-degree F oven for 20-25 minutes.

Makes about 6 servings

A great side dish for any meal

Five Bean Bake

1/2 cup of bacon or side pork, cut into small pieces
1 small onion, diced
1/2 lb. of brown sugar
1 can of kidney beans, drained
1 can of wax beans, drained
1 can of green beans, drained
1 can of pork and beans, undrained

Method: Brown bacon or side pork and drain off grease. Combine all other ingredients and put into a lightly greased baking dish and bake 1 hour at 350-degree F.

All beans except the pork and beans may come
fresh from your garden

Vickie Owens

Sweet Potato Casserole

4 large sweet potatoes
1 stick of butter, melted
1 1/2 cups of milk
2 eggs
1/2 cup of powdered sugar
1 cup of marshmallows
1/2 cup of walnuts, chopped
2 tsp of vanilla
1 tsp of cinnamon
1 tsp of nutmeg

Method: Boil sweet potatoes until soft. Mash sweet potatoes, blend in vanilla, brown sugar, eggs, cinnamon, and nutmeg. Stir in milk.

Bake in 2 1/2-quart baking dish at 350-degree F for 30 minutes. The last five minutes' layer marshmallows on top of casserole and sprinkle with chopped walnuts. Bake this until marshmallows are a golden brown.

This recipe goes good with sugar cured ham

Potato Casserole

5 lbs. of red or white potatoes, cooked
8 oz. cream cheese
1 1/2 cups of milk
1/2 cup of butter
1 tsp of garlic salt
Paprika

Method: Cook potatoes as mentioned, mash the potatoes and add all other ingredients except paprika. Put in a lightly buttered baking dish, sprinkle with paprika and bake at 350-degree F for about 20 minutes.

You can also top potatoes with cheddar cheese

Hash Brown Casserole

2 lbs. of frozen hash browns
1 can of cream of celery soup
1 can of cream of chicken soup
8 oz. sour cream
1 small onion, finely chopped
1 stick of melted butter

Method: Mix all ingredients and bake at 375-degree F in lightly greased baking dish for about 30 minutes.

Crush potato chips or crackers over the top when you take out of the oven.

A take along casserole for any occasion

Cheesy Potato Bake

Use potatoes to your family size serving. Scrub potatoes and cut into chunks.

Cover the bottom of baking dish with raw bacon slices. Now fill with potatoes.

Sprinkle with salt and pepper to your taste.

Cover with cheese slices.

Top cheese with raw bacon slices.

Bake at 350-degree F for 1 hour or until potatoes are tender and done.

This can be served with breakfast, lunch, or dinner

Vickie Owens

Potato-Burger Casserole

Raw potatoes peeled and sliced to family size
1 lb. of hamburger
1 small onion, sliced
Rutabaga, sliced
Cabbage, sliced
1 can of mushroom soup
1 can of vegetable beef soup

Method: Butter the bottom of a 9x13" pan. Cover the bottom of the pan with your sliced potatoes, about 1-inch-deep with potatoes. Crumble raw hamburger over the potatoes. Spread raw sliced rutabaga and sliced cabbage on top of hamburger. Pour mushroom and vegetable soup over the top. Bake at 350-degree F for 1-1 1/2 hours or until the center of casserole is done.

This should make a hearty meal of the day

Chop-Away Casserole

Pork chops-About 6
5 red potatoes, peeled and sliced
2 small onions, peeled and sliced
1 green pepper, diced
Spiced herbs of your choice
1 can of cream of celery soup

Method: Fry pork chops until brown on both sides. Line the bottom of a greased 9x13" pan with browned pork chops. Cover pork chops with potatoes, onion and green pepper. Salt and pepper to taste and add your favorite spiced herbs. Cover with a can of cream of celery soup. Bake at 350-degree F for 1 hour.

This is a one-dish dinner for all

Vickie Owens

Beefy Mushroom Casserole

2 lbs. of stewing meat, cut into small pieces
1 can of cream of mushroom soup
1 can of French onion soup
1 can of cream of onion soup
1 jar of buttered mushrooms

Method: Mix all ingredients together and put in a lightly buttered baking dish.

Bake at 350-degree F for 1-1/2 hours. Stir every 20 minutes. Make sure the meat is tender before serving.

Serve with mashed potatoes or over fresh boiled potatoes

Spinach Bake

3 eggs
6 Tbsp. of whole wheat flour
1 lb. of fresh spinach, torn into pieces
2 cups of cottage cheese
2 cups of grated cheddar cheese
1/2 tsp of salt
Wheat germ

Method: Beat eggs and flour until smooth. Add all remaining ingredients and mix well. Pour into a well-greased baking dish. Sprinkle with wheat germ and cheese. Bake at 350-degree F for 45 minutes.

A perfectly healthy casserole

Vickie Owens

Asparagus Loaf

1 cup of soda cracker crumbs, crushed fine
2 eggs, beaten
4 Tbsp. of butter
2 cups of hot milk, not boiled
4 cups of asparagus, fresh out of the garden, chopped
1 tsp of salt

Method: Cut asparagus in 1" pieces. Mix together all ingredients and pour into a lightly oiled bread pan. Bake about 40 minutes or until set.

You will be surprised how wonderful this taste

Beef Pot Pie

1 can of beef
2 cans of water
2 potatoes, diced
1 tsp of salt
Dash of pepper

Pot Pie Dough

2 cups of flour
2 Tbsp. of lard
1/2 tsp of salt
Water

Method: Blend flour, lard and salt evenly, add just enough water to form a pie dough. Roll out and cut into a thin circle and then cut into 2" squares. Drop into the boiling broth mixture from above. Stir well. Reduce heat and cook about 20 minutes. This can be made ahead of time. The longer it cooks the better the flavor. This can be served in bowls.

This recipe should serve 4-6 people

Vickie Owens

Skillet Fry

Carrots, chopped
1 onion, chopped
Dry bread crumbs
Salt and pepper to taste
Bacon grease

Method: Vary proportions on the number of people being served.

Wash carrots, chop and cook 10-12 minutes in bacon grease. Add onion and dry bread crumbs, and salt and pepper to taste. Cover skillet and let steam about 1/2 hour. Keep stirring to mix well.

The Best Dressing

2 loaves of bread, cubed and dried
1 small onion, chopped fine
1-2 Tbsp. of sage, to taste
1 stick of melted butter
1 cooked turkey gizzard, chopped
1 cooked turkey liver, chopped
1 cooked turkey heart, chopped
Salt and pepper to taste
Broth from the already baked turkey
2-3 cups of hot water

Method: Mix all ingredients together. Dressing should be moist. If not moist enough add a little hot water. You may also add more sage, salt and pepper to finalize the taste. Stuff turkey and bake at 350-degree F for 1 hour. You may also put dressing in a lightly buttered baking dish and bake for 1 hour.

You may add diced apples, diced celery,
or whole cranberries for extra flavor

Vickie Owens

Frozen Vegetable Cheese Bake

4 cups of mixed frozen vegetables
I prefer broccoli, cauliflower and carrots
1 16 oz. jar of Velveeta cheese
1 10oz can of cream of mushroom soup
Dried French onions

Method: Steam frozen vegetables until almost tender. Slow cook cheese and soup on low heat until creamy. Add vegetables to cheese and soup mixture. Mix well. Place in 8x12" baking dish and smother with dried French onions. Bake at 350-degree F for about 15 minutes.

This makes a lovely holiday casserole
You may choose frozen vegetables of your choice

Goulash

1 box of elbow or shell macaroni
1 lb. of hamburger
1/2 onion, finely chopped
2 12oz cans of tomato sauce
1/4 cup of green pepper, finely chopped
Salt and pepper to taste
Shredded cheddar cheese

Method: Cook macaroni until tender, drain. Cook hamburger and onion until hamburger is browned and onion tender and drain. Mix hamburger, onion, tomato sauce, green pepper, salt and pepper. Mix everything together well. Put in baking dish, cover with shredded cheddar cheese and bake at 350-degree F until cheese is melted. About 15 minutes

Serve while hot with garlic bread
For extra great taste, sprinkle sugar atop the goulash

Tuna & Noodle Casserole

4 cups of egg noodles
1 tsp of salt
2 10 oz. cans of tuna, drained
1 can of cream of chicken soup
1 small can of baby sweet peas
1 cup of shredded cheddar cheese
1/2 cup milk
16-20 crackers, crushed

Method: Boil water and add 1Tbsp. of salt to water, add egg noodles and cook until noodles are tender, about 15 minutes. Drain noodles, add the rest of the ingredients to noodles and mix well. Should be creamy. Place in a lightly buttered casserole dish.

Place casserole in oven covered with cracker crumbs and bake at 350-degree F for about 15 minutes.

Chicken Delight Casserole

1 10 oz. can of white chicken, drained
1 8 oz. pkg. of cream cheese, softened
2 pkgs. of crescent rolls, 8 each
1 large can of cream of chicken soup, family size
2 small cans of chicken broth
1 small box of minute rice

Method. Mix cream of chicken soup and chicken broth on top of stove, stirring constantly to form a gravy.

Mix softened cream cheese and chicken together

Roll out crescent rolls, fill each crescent roll with chicken mixture and wrap. Lay out in a lightly buttered baking dish and cover with half of chicken gravy. Bake at 350-degree F until biscuits become golden brown.

While these are baking make minute rice to directions on box.

When all is done place rice on serving plate, add a couple chicken biscuits and cover with gravy.

Should serve 6-8 people depending on the amount of rice cooked.

Vickie Owens

Yam Casserole

2 yams, peeled and cubed
2 apples, peeled and cubed
1 small onion, sliced thin
1/2 cup of brown sugar
1 lb. of cooked sausage, cut in chunks
2 Tbsp. of vegetable oil

Method: Preheat oven to 400-degree F. Grease a 9x13" baking dish. Combine potatoes, apples, onion and oil in a large bowl. Stir until well coated. Place in baking dish and bake covered for 30 minutes. Add sausage cubes and bake 10 minutes longer.

Makes 6 servings

Hamburger Pie Casserole

1 lb. of ground beef, browned and drained
1/4 cup of onion, chopped
1 can of cream of celery soup
1 1/2 cups of cheddar cheese, shredded
1 can of French style green beans
10-12 potatoes
1/4 tsp of salt
1/4 tsp of pepper
1/2 cup of milk
1/4 cup of butter

Method: Brown hamburger and onion and drain. Add cream of celery soup and 1 can of French style green beans to hamburger/onion mixture. Boil potatoes until done, mash potatoes adding, salt, pepper, milk and butter until potatoes are fluffy.

In a 9x13" baking dish place hamburger mixture on bottom, top with mashed potatoes, cover mashed potatoes with 1 1/2 cups of cheddar cheese and place in oven at 350-degree F for about 15 minutes, until cheese is fully melted.

This is a great meal, and makes a wonderful left over

Vickie Owens

VEGETABLES

Vickie Owens

Baked Beans

2-16oz cans of pork and beans
1 cup of brown sugar
1 lb. of bacon cut into small pieces
1/2 tsp of dry mustard
1/2 cup of ketchup
1 medium onion, finely chopped

Method: Mix all ingredients and bake uncovered at 350-degree F for 60 minutes or until desired thickness.

Baked beans are everyone's favorite
Great taste in the iron skillet in the oven

Modern day-throw them in your crock pot

Garlicky Green Beans

1 lb. of fresh green beans
6 Tbsp. of butter
1/2 cup of onion, finely chopped
1 tsp of garlic powder
Salt and pepper to taste

Method: Cook fresh green beans in salted water until tender, drain. In a skillet sauté onion in butter until tender. Add garlic powder. Add cooked green beans to skillet and toss. Season with salt and pepper to taste. If you like more garlic go ahead and add more and toss.

You may also add fresh sliced mushrooms in with the sauté onions. Ham is good to add as well

Saucy Green Beans

1 1/2 cups of sugar
1 cup of vinegar
3/4 cup of water
1lb of fresh green beans

Method: Boil the first three ingredients 5 minutes and pour over the fresh cooked green beans.

The first three ingredient mixture is also very good poured over sliced cucumbers.

If you haven't tried them, they are a must

Quick Pickles from the Garden

7 cucumbers
1 cup of onion, sliced thin
1 cup of green pepper, diced
2 cups of sugar
1 cup of vinegar
2 Tbsp. of salt
1 tsp of celery seed

Method: Cut cucumbers, onion and green pepper. Combine sugar, vinegar, salt and celery seed. Mix well.

Pour vinegar mixture over pickles. Cover and refrigerate 5 days before serving.

Stir twice each day for the five days. Don't forget! Ready to serve on the 6th day.

You will love these if you love cucumbers

Steamed Kale

1 lb. of kale
2 tsp of oil
2 cloves of garlic, peeled and cut up
1/3 cup of water

Method: Wash kale well, cut off and discard the tough stems.

Heat oil in large iron skillet, or regular skillet. Add the garlic and cook it for 20-30 seconds. Add the water and bring to a boil. Put kale in water and cover skillet, let steam for about 8 minutes. Kale will be tender and bright green in color.

Kale is very healthy for you

Cabbage Fry

1 Tbsp. of oil
1 large onion, chopped
1 lb. of cabbage, cored and thinly sliced
1 apple, thinly sliced
Pepper to taste
1 Tbsp. of brown sugar
1 cup of warm water
1 Tbsp. of vinegar

Method: Heat oil in cast iron skillet, or any skillet, add onion and cook about 1 minute. Add cabbage and apple and cook about 5 minutes. Combine pepper, brown sugar, water and vinegar. Add this to the cabbage/onion mixture in skillet. Cook covered on low heat for about 20 minutes, stirring every 5 minutes until done.

This can be served hot or cold

Vickie Owens

Stuffed Cabbage

1 solid head of cabbage
Thin white sauce
Bread crumbs
Paprika

Method: Shred cabbage. Fill a well-oiled baking dish with alternate layers of cabbage and white sauce. Cover with buttered bread crumbs. Sprinkle with paprika. Cover baking dish and bake at 350-degree F for about 35 to 40 minutes.

This is great served with boiled or baked ham
You can add ham chunks to the bake for extra flavor

Creamed Potatoes

2 1/2 lbs. of potatoes, preferably from your garden
1 stick of salted butter
3 cups of milk
Salt to taste
1/2 cup of flour
1/2 cup of cheese, cut up, any kind
1/2 cup of ham, cut up in chunks

Method: Slice potatoes and cook in salted water in kettle until tender. Drain off water. Place potatoes in a buttered baking dish, in same kettle, melt butter, add flour, and about 3 cups of milk to make gravy. Add cut up cheese and ham to this gravy. Pour this mixture over potatoes in baking dish and bake at 350-degree F until bubbling and turning brown on top.

Vickie Owens

Wonderful Potatoes

5 lbs. of potatoes
1 tsp of onion salt
1/2 tsp of celery salt
1 cup of sour cream
1/4 tsp of pepper
1/4 cup of butter

Method: Cook potatoes until done. Drain and mash. Add sour cream, butter, onion, salt, celery salt and pepper. Beat and then whip until fluffy.

Scrape into lightly buttered baking dish, sprinkle with butter and paprika.

Bake at 350-degree F until heated through, about 20 minutes.

Quick and Easy Potatoes

6 medium raw potatoes, thinly sliced
1 stick of butter
Salt and pepper
2 cups of milk
2 Tbsp. of corn starch

Method: Place sliced potatoes in a greased baking dish. Combine milk, butter, salt, pepper and cornstarch, stirring constantly until comes to a boil and smooth. Pour over potatoes in baking dish and bake at 375-degree F for one hour.

You may also add diced ham to these

Apple-Carrot Bake

8 carrots, sliced and cooked, fresh from the garden
5 large baking apples, sliced
5 Tbsp. of sugar
2 1/2 Tbsp. of flour
1/2 tsp of nutmeg
1/2 cup of orange juice
3 Tbsp. of butter

Method: Alternate apples and carrots in a lightly greased baking dish. Combine flour, sugar, nutmeg and orange juice. Pour this mixture over the apples and carrots. Dot with butter. Bake at 350-degree F for about 40-45 minutes.

This is great served with baked ham or pork chops
It is always fun to try something new and easy

Glazed Carrots

4 medium carrots, sliced
2 Tbsp. of butter
2 Tbsp. of sugar

Method: Wash and scrape carrots, slice to desired bite size pieces. Cook in boiling salt water until tender and drain. Melt butter and sugar in frying pan, add carrots and cook until browned and glazed.

You may also substitute brown sugar for sugar

Vickie Owens

Scalloped Corn with Green Peppers

2 cups of canned corn, drained
1 Green pepper, minced
1/2 cup of bread crumbs
1 egg, well beaten
1 cup of medium white sauce
1 tsp of sugar

Method: Combine white sauce and egg, beat well. Add corn, sugar and green pepper. Pour into well oiled baking dish. Cover with bread crumbs and bake at 425-degree F until golden brown.

Should server 6

Great side dish for the holidays

Scalloped Corn

2 cups of canned corn, drained
1/2 cup of bread crumbs
1 egg, well beaten
1 tsp of sugar
1/2 tsp of salt
3/4 cup of milk

Method: Combine eggs and milk and beat thoroughly. Add corn, sugar and salt. Pour into a greased baking dish. Cover with bread crumbs and bake at 425-degree F until golden brown on top.

Tired of the same old vegetables at your table?
Try scalloped corn
Very delicious

Vickie Owens

Baked Corn

2 cups of canned corn
2 eggs, well beaten
1 Tbsp. of butter
2 tsp of flour
2 Tbsp. of milk
2 Tbsp. of cram
1 tsp of salt

Method: Combine all ingredients and mix thoroughly. Pour into a well-greased baking dish. Bake at 400-degree F until an inserted knife comes out clean. If needed, additional milk can be added.

Add some color to your plate. They say,
"The more colorful the plate, the healthier the meal."

Creamed Peas

2 cups of sweet peas, drained
1 Tbsp. of butter
Milk
Flour
Water
Salt
Pepper

Method: Put peas in medium size sauce pan, add 1 Tbsp. of butter and cover peas with milk. While the peas are starting to come to a boil mix flour and water into a smooth, thick mixture. Add the flour and water to the peas until the peas come to a nice smooth, thickened consistency. Add salt and pepper to taste. Mix well.

You may also add new small red potatoes and ham to these

Vickie Owens

Sugar Snap Peas

1 lb. of sugar snap peas, from garden
1/2 of a small white onion, thinly sliced
1 clove of garlic, minced
1 pinch of sugar
1/3 cup of oil, olive oil if you have it
1/4 tsp of pepper

Method: Heat pot of water to boil. Add peas and cook one minute. Drain and rinse peas under cold water. Place peas in a bowl. Add onion, sugar, olive oil, and pepper. Toss and refrigerate about 1/2 hour before serving.

Serves about 6 people

Sugar snap peas have a wonderful taste
Great summer dish

Just Kraut

1 large can of sauerkraut
1/2 tsp of sugar
1 large Tbsp. of flour
1/4 cup of cold water

Method: Heat un-drained sauerkraut in your iron skillet or regular skillet with 1/2 tsp of sugar, stir. Next add 1 large Tbsp. of flour, mixed with 1/4 cup of cold water. Stir good and heat through until Kraut is hot and steamy.

This sauerkraut has a different delicious taste
Only meant for you Kraut lovers

Sauerkraut Bake

1 quart of sauerkraut, drained
1 quart of tomatoes
1 cup of brown sugar
1/2 lb. of bacon, cut into small pieces

Method: Mix all ingredients together and bake at 350-degree F, uncovered for about 2 1/2 hours.

This goes great with spare ribs, boil them up
and throw them over the top of your kraut

Also good with short ribs on the side

Grandma sometimes added cut up polish sausage to the kraut

Beets in Vinegar

Hopefully your beets will be home grown, fresh out of the garden

Wash beets thoroughly, leaving 3" of stems and the roots attached.

Put in pot, cover with water and boil until tender. Drain, cover with cold water and slip skins and roots from beets.

Slice, add vinegar, salt and sugar to taste. Let stand one hour and serve.

        This is the fast, easy way to serve beets
        Beets are rich in color and flavor

Pickled Beets

3 lbs. of beets cooked tender, peeled, diced or sliced
Save beat juice from cooking and add 1 cup of water, 1 cup of vinegar, 1/2 cup of brown sugar, 2 tsp of salt, 1 tsp of cinnamon, and 12 cloves.

Bring beat juice to boil, take off stove and remove the cloves. Pour over diced or sliced beets. Let cool and refrigerate

You may also put these in pint or quart jars
and keep refrigerated

Squash

Pumpkin Squash
Winter Squash
Acorn Squash

Method: Choose whichever squash you like, pare and cut into squares

Place in a well buttered casserole dish with alternate layers of brown sugar and butter.

Bake at 375-degree F

Cover with tin foil when baking and bake for about 35 to 40 minutes or until tender

1 squash may serve between 4-6 people depending on the helping size.

Another colorful, healthy, vegetable for your table

Vickie Owens

Cheesy Asparagus

2 cups of asparagus
2 Tbsp. of melted butter
4 eggs
1/4 cup of grated cheese
Salt and pepper to taste

Method: Cut asparagus into 1" chunks, add butter and cook on top of stove about 3-4 minutes. Add eggs and season to taste. Sprinkle with cheese and cook until the egg whites are firm.

This would make an excellent breakfast dish
Eggs, asparagus, toast and orange juice

Kohlrabi

Kohlrabi-Wash thoroughly, trim roots and peel

This can be shred raw and used in salads or slaw

To Cook: boil or steam kohlrabi for 15 to 20 minutes, or until tender and cover with melted cheese.

Kohlrabi may also be used in soups, stews, or for baking.

Kohlrabi is full of nutrients and minerals like copper, potassium, manganese, iron, and calcium, as well as vitamins, such as vitamin C, B-complex vitamins, vitamin A, and vitamin K. Kohlrabi is also high in dietary fiber and antioxidant compounds

Healthy, Healthy, Healthy!

Vickie Owens

Creamed Onions

2 jars of whole onions
1 can of cream of celery soup

Method: Combine onions and cream of celery soup and put in casserole dish. Place in oven at 350-degree F for about 15-20 minutes or until heated through.

Very simple side dish

I

Sweet Onion Bake

4 large Vidalia onions, cut in half
1/4 cup of honey
1 Tbsp. of soy sauce

Method: Brush onions with honey and soy sauce mixture. Bake at 350-degree F until onions are tender.

Serves 4

Eggplant Delight

3 medium eggplant
2 Tbsp. of butter
1 cup of onion, chopped
2 garlic cloves, minced
1/2 lb. mushrooms, chopped
1 cup of cooked rice
Salt and pepper to taste
1 cup of cottage cheese, I prefer small curd

Method: Slice eggplants lengthwise in half. Scoop out inside with spoon down to about 1/4" inch of the skin. Chop the eggplant innards that you scooped out with a spoon and cook in a hot skillet with butter, onions garlic, and mushrooms over medium heat until the onions are clear and the eggplant is soft. Combine all other ingredients and stuff the eggplant. Bake uncovered at 350-degree F for 40 minutes.

Makes 6 servings

Fried Eggplant

Slice medium eggplant and soak in salt water for about 1/2 hour. Drain water off eggplant.

Pat eggplant dry.

Dip eggplant in beaten eggs, roll in flour, dip in cracker crumbs.

Brown in lightly oil, hot iron skillet or frying pan.

Baked Eggplant

1 medium eggplant
1/4 cup of butter
1/2 cup of bread crumbs
1 tsp minced onion
2 eggs, well beaten
Salt and pepper to taste

Method: Pare eggplant and cut into 1/4" slices. Cook in salted boiling water until tender. Drain and mash. Season with salt and pepper to taste, mix thoroughly. Pour into well-greased baking dish and bake at 400 degrees F until well heated and browned.

Yummy Brussels Sprouts

1 lb. of Brussels sprouts cooked 5-10 minutes
1/2 tsp of garlic powder
1/2 tsp of pepper
1/3 cup of vinegar
1/2 tsp of mustard
1/2 cup of oil

Method: Mix all dressing ingredients in jar and shake well. Pour over Brussels sprouts while still warm. Refrigerate 4 hours before serving.

Turnip Greens

2 cups of turnip greens
1 small onion, sliced
Garlic to taste
1 Tbsp. of butter

Method: Take a little bacon grease, and your small onion and fry until onion is golden brown. Add 1 Tbsp. of butter, garlic to taste and add turnip greens.

Simmer about 20 minutes adding hot water as you go so they do not burn. The water will slowly cook off and after 20 minutes you will have the best tasting turnip greens you have ever eaten.

Wilted Greens

Use Dandelion Greens
Mustard Greens
Kale or Beet Greens

Method: Use any kind of the above three greens that you like. Clean the brown leaves off.

Wash several times thoroughly under cold water to clean.

Put desired amount in frying pan, but do not add water.

Cook until wilted, add fresh butter, salt and pepper to taste. Let butter melt through greens and serve hot with any meal.

Vickie Owens

PIES, CAKES, & FROSTINGS

Vickie Owens

Gooseberry Pie

3 cups of gooseberries, picked from bush and cleaned.
1 1/2 cups of sugar, or sugar to taste
2 Tbsp. of corn starch, used for pie thickening

Method: Stem and wash gooseberries in cold water. Put gooseberries in sauce pan and cover with water. Cook until they come to a boil, turn stove down and continue to cook, stirring constantly. Let cool until thickened.

Take off stove and add sugar to desired taste. Pour into a 9" homemade pie shell. Sprinkle with corn starch. Put crisscross top crust on, brush with butter and sprinkle with sugar. Bake at 350-degree F on spill pan for about 20-25 minutes.

This is great served warm with vanilla ice cream,
or evaporated milk poured over the top

Cream Pie

3/4 cup of sugar
1/3 cup of flour
1/8 tsp of salt
2 cups of scalded milk
1/2 tsp of vanilla flavoring
2 Tbsp. of butter
2 eggs, well beaten

Method: Combine butter, sugar, salt, flour and eggs. Add milk slowly, stirring constantly. Cook over hot water until thick and smooth. Add vanilla flavoring. Bake at 350-degree F for about 40 minutes.

Grandma's Rhubarb Pie

1 egg, well beaten
1 cup of sugar
Pinch of salt
1 cup finely chopped rhubarb
1/2 cup cracker crumbs
1/2 cup chopped raisons
2 Tbsp. of melted butter

Method: Combine sugar and eggs; add rhubarb, cracker crumbs, a few grains of salt, raisons and butter. Mix thoroughly. Pour into a 9" homemade pie crust, cover top with crust and slice holes in top crust. Brush top crust with butter and sprinkle with sugar. Bake at 350-degree F on pie dripping pan for about 45 minutes.

Let cool and serve

Squash Pie

2 cups of squash
1 can evaporated milk
1/4 cup of sugar
1 Tbsp. of flour
1/4 tsp of ground cinnamon

Method: Mix all ingredients together and pour into a 9" homemade pie crust. Bake at 350-degree F in preheated oven for 45-60 minutes.

Squash pie is like pumpkin pie, test the center for firmness and doneness.

Great served with cool whip for
Thanksgiving Dinner

Blackberry Jam Pie

3 eggs
1/2 cup of sugar
1 cup of sour cream
1 Tbsp. of melted butter
1 cup of blackberry jam
1 Tbsp. of cornstarch
1 dash of salt

Method: Beat egg yolks until thick, add sour cream, butter and corn starch. Add blackberry jam, sugar and salt; mix well. Pour into a 9" homemade pie crust. Bake at 425-degree F for about 25 minutes.

Cover pie with meringue

Meringue

3 egg whites, 3 Tbsp. of sugar, 1 tsp vanilla
Beat until stiff peaks form
Smooth on pie and bake at 325-degree F
For about 15-20 minutes
Watch closely, until meringue is golden brown

Pecan Pie

1-9" homemade crust pie shell
3 eggs
1/4 tsp of salt
3/4 cup of sugar
1/2 cup of melted butter
1 cup of dark corn syrup
1 1/2 cups of pecan halve

Method: Bake your pie shell in oven at 450-degree F for five minutes, let cool.

Beat eggs and salt until very light and lemon colored. Beat in sugar a little at a time. With a wire whisk fold in melted butter and corn syrup. Pour into partially baked pie shell and arrange pecan halves on top of pie. Bake for10 minutes in preheated 425-degree F oven, reduce heat to 325-degree F and bake 30 minutes longer.

Let cool and serve

Vickie Owens

Sour Cream Raison Pie

1-9" homemade pie crust
2 eggs
3/4 cup of sugar
1/4 tsp of salt
1 tsp of cinnamon
1/2 tsp of nutmeg
1/3 tsp of cloves
1 cup of sour cream
1 cup of seeded raisons

Method: Prepare pie crust and refrigerate while you make the pie filling. Beat eggs lightly, stir in sugar, salt, cinnamon, nutmeg, and cloves. Next stir in sour cream and raisons. Pour into chilled pie crust. Bake at 450-degree F for 10 minutes. Reduce heat to 350-degree F and bake 30 minutes longer, or until knife inserted into center of pie comes out clean.

Best served warm

Rhubarb Custard Pie

2 cups of rhubarb, finely chopped
1 1/4 cups of sugar
2 Tbsp. of flour
1 Tbsp. of cornstarch
2 Tbsp. of butter
2 egg yolks, beaten
1 tsp of vanilla
1 9" homemade baked pie shell

Method: Mix first seven ingredients, or in order given. Let stand 30 minutes; mixture will look thickened. Pour into pie shell with a top crust and bake at 375-degree F for about 45 minutes, placed on a drip pan. Remove from oven.

Cover top with meringue and pop back in oven for about 15 minutes at 325-degree F, watch closely until meringue turns a golden brown

Vickie Owens

Blackberry or Black Raspberry Pie

Pastry for a 2-crust pie, prefer homemade pastry
4 cups of blackberries or black raspberries
3 Tbsp. of flour
1/4 cup of sugar
1 Tbsp. of lemon juice
1 Tbsp. of butter

Method: Line pie pan with first crust and brush with butter.

Mix rest of ingredients and toss lightly. Fill pie shell with tossed ingredients.

Cut out designs in second crust and lay over top of pie. Pinch around edges to seal crusts together. Brush top with butter, and sprinkle with sugar.

Put pie on tray to catch drippings and bake at 350-degree F for about 20-25 minutes or until pie crust is golden brown.

Let cool before serving

Very good with evaporated milk poured over the top

Onion and Cheese Pie

1 1/4 cups freshly rolled cracker crumbs
1 stick of butter
1 1/4 cups of milk
2 1/2 cups of onions, thinly sliced
3 eggs
1 tsp of salt
1/4 tsp of pepper
1/4 lb. of sharp grated cheddar cheese
1 Tbsp. of chopped ripe olives

Method: Mix together the freshly rolled cracker crumbs and butter, pat on the bottom and sides of a 9" pie pan.

Mix the rest of the ingredients well and put in pie shell. Bake at 350-degree F oven for about 25-30 minutes.

May serve with fresh sliced sweet onions
across the top

Country Cowboy Cake

1 6 oz. can of pork and beans, drained
1 8oz can crushed pineapple with juice
2 cups of sugar
2 cups of flour
2 tsp of cinnamon
1/2 tsp of salt
2 tsp of baking soda
1 tsp of baking powder
1 cup of oil
4 eggs

Method: Mash beans and pineapple with pineapple juice. Add rest of ingredients and mix well. Pour into a 9x13' greased and floured cake pan. Bake at 350-degree F for 35 minutes. This cake freezes well.

Let cool and frost with cream cheese frosting

Cream Cheese Frosting

1 stick of butter
1 lb. of powdered sugar
1 tsp of vanilla
1 8oz pkg. of cream cheese
Blend butter and cream cheese. Add powdered sugar and vanilla, blend until smooth.

Granny's Pumpkin Cake

3 1/2 cups of flour
2 tsp of cinnamon
2 tsp of nutmeg
2/3 cup of water
4 eggs
3 cups of sugar
2 cups of cooked pumpkin
1/2 cup of raisons

Method: Mix together dry ingredients. Add the rest of the ingredients and mix until smooth. Bake in a 9x13" greased and floured cake pan at 350-degree F for 35-40 minutes. Test with toothpick in center of cake for doneness.

Frost with powdered sugar or cream cheese frosting, sprinkle with crushed walnuts

Vickie Owens

Granny's Silly Eyed Pumpkin Pie

Homemade pie shell for a 10" pie shell

2 cups of pumpkin, cooked and mashed
4 eggs, yolks only, save whites for pie
1 cup of sugar
1/2 tsp of cinnamon
1/2 cup of butter, melted
1/2 cup of whiskey, straight from the still
1/3 cup of whipping cream
1 Tbsp. of cornstarch

Method: Beat together pumpkin, sugar, cinnamon and egg yolks. Stir in melted butter, whiskey and whipping cream. Beat egg whites until stiff and add cornstarch to egg whites, blending well. Fold egg whites into pumpkin mixture and mix well. Pour in a 10" pie shell and bake at 375-degree F for about 1 hour. Center of pie should be firm when done.

Enjoy-Don't get silly-eyed!

Applesauce Cake

1/2 cup lard or shortening
1 1/2 cups of thick sweet applesauce
1 tsp of baking soda
1 cup of sugar
4 eggs, well beaten
1/4 cup of sour milk
2 1/2 cups of flour
1 tsp of nutmeg
3/4 tsp of salt

Method: Cream lard and sugar. Add eggs and applesauce. Beat thoroughly. Sift flour, baking soda, salt and spices. Add alternately with milk to shortening and sugar mixture. Pour into a well-greased loaf pan. Bake at 375-degree F for about 45 minutes.

Let cool about 5 minutes and take from pan and continue cooling on wire rack for about 1/2 hour.

Slice and serve

Nana's Skillet Cake

3 cups of flour
2 cups of sugar
3 Tbsp. of cocoa
1 tsp of salt
2 tsp of baking soda
2 Tbsp. of vinegar
1/4 lb. of butter, melted
2 cups of cold water

Method: Preheat oven to 375-degree F. Grease 12" iron skillet. Sift flour, sugar, cocoa, salt and baking soda into skillet. After stirring dry ingredients together take a wood spoon and make 3 holes in the dry ingredients. Pour vanilla in one hole, vinegar into the 2nd hole, and melted butter into the third and last hole. Pour the cold water over all the mixture and stir. Bake for 25 minutes at 375-degree F.

Icing

1/8 lb. butter
2/3 cup brown sugar
1/2 to 2/3 cup ground walnut
3 Tbsp. of canned milk or 2 Tbsp. of whole milk
Melt butter in sauce pan, stir in brown sugar. Add walnuts and canned milk or whole milk. Stir well. Pour this over cake when done and put in broiler for about 5 minutes or until top bubbles.

Front Porch Cake

1/2 cup of butter
1-2/3 cup of sugar
2-1/4 cups of flour
3 tsp of baking powder
1 cup of water
4 egg whites, beaten stiff
Flavoring

Method: Cream butter and sugar. Sift baking powder with flour. Add flour and water, alternating a little at a time. Fold in egg whites and the last of the flour. Add your flavoring.

Bake in a greased and floured 9x13" cake pan at 350-degree F for 30-35 minutes or until done.

Your choice of frosting

Vickie Owens

Hard Times Cake

1 1/2 cups of butter
2 cups of sugar
1 cup of sour cream
3 cups of flour
3 eggs
1/2 tsp of baking soda

Method: Mix all ingredients together. Bake in layers and spread with any flavor of jelly when cool.

A quick fix for your sweet tooth

Tomato Soup Cake

2 cups of flour, sifted
1 tsp of baking soda
2 tsp of baking powder
1 tsp of cinnamon
1 tsp of nutmeg
1/2 tsp of cloves
1/2 cup of shortening
1 cup of sugar
1 can of tomato soup
1 cup of walnuts, chopped
1 cup of raisons

Method: Sift dry ingredients 3 times. Cream shortening and sugar until creamy and fluffy. Add dry ingredients and soup alternately. Stir in nuts and raisins. Mix all by hand. Pour in greased and floured loaf pan. Bake 50-60 minutes at 350-degree F. Let stand 24 hours before cutting.

Cream cheese frosting is optional

Graham Cracker Cake

1 1/2 cups of butter
1 cup of sugar
3 eggs
2 tsp of baking powder
3/4 cup of milk
1 tsp of vanilla
1 cup of chopped walnuts
1 lb. of graham crackers

Method: Cream butter and sugar. Add egg yolks and beat thoroughly. Combine with graham cracker crumbs rolled out very fine. Add baking powder to mixture. Add vanilla, milk and nuts. Mix well. Beat egg whites until stiff and add to mixture. Pour into well-greased shallow pans. Bake at 375-degree F for about 30 minutes.

Serve with whipped cream

Mayonnaise Cake

2 cups of flour
1 cup of sugar
2 tsp of baking soda
1/4 tsp of salt
1/2 cup of cocoa
1 cup of Miracle Whip or mayonnaise
1 cup of water
1 tsp of vanilla

Method: Combine flour, sugar, baking soda, salt and cocoa. Hand stir. Add miracle whip, water and vanilla. Beat until smooth. Pour into a greased and lightly floured 9x13" cake pan. Bake at 350-degree F for 30-40 minutes or until cake pulls away from the sides of the pan.

Very moist chocolate cake

Everyone's Favorite

Butter Cake

1/2 cup of butter
1 cup of sugar
2 eggs
3/4 cup of milk
2 cups of flour
2 tsp of baking powder
1/4 tsp of salt
1 tsp of vanilla

Method: Cream together butter and milk and add sugar gradually. Sift flour, baking powder, soda and salt. Add alternately with milk to butter-sugar mixture.

Pour into a 9x13" cake pan well-greased and floured and bake at 350-degree F for 30-35 minutes or until done in center when checked with a toothpick. Toothpick should come out clean.

Blueberry Best

Wash blueberries just before using and remove stems.

2 cups of blueberries or you can use raspberries
1/2 cup of sugar
1 egg, well beaten
1 1/2 cups of flour
1 tsp of baking powder
1/2 cup of milk
1/2 cup of butter, melted

Method: Preheat oven to 425-degree F. Combine berries, sugar and egg in a greased baking dish. Combine flour, baking powder and sugar in a mixing bowl. Mix egg, milk and melted butter together. Stir gently into the flour mixture. Spread over top of berries and bake at 350-degree F for 30 minutes.

Let cool and serve

Chocolate Frosting

2 squares of unsweetened chocolate
2 Tbsp. of softened butter
1/2 tsp of vanilla
Pinch of salt
1 cup of confectioners' sugar
1 egg
1/3 cup of milk

Method: Melt chocolate over hot, not boiling water. Combine butter, vanilla, and salt in mixing bowl. Stir in confectioners' sugar a little at a time until smooth. Heat eggs in milk and melted chocolate. Beat hard until creamy and stiff enough to spread.

Maple Frosting

2 cups of confectioners' sugar
Pinch of salt
1 Tbsp. of softened butter
3 Tbsp. of maple syrup
1 Tbsp. of heavy cream

Method: Combine all ingredients and beat until mixture is smooth and of spreading consistency. A great frosting for carrot cake. May add crushed walnuts on top of the frosting on cake.

Butter Cream Frosting

1/2 cup of softened butter
1 1/2 cups of confectioners' sugar
1/2 tsp of vanilla
Milk

Method: Combine all ingredients adding a little milk at a time until you get the consistency you want for cake spreading. If frosting is too thin, add more confectioners' sugar to thicken. For coffee butter cream add 1 tsp of instant coffee instead of the vanilla.

Butter cream frosting is good on any cake
Need more...double the recipe

Vickie Owens

DESSERTS

Vickie Owens

Raison Apple Bake

1 cup of raisons
1/2 cup of brown sugar
4 cups of pared, quartered apples
1/4 cup of water
1 Tbsp. of butter
1/4 tsp of salt
1/4 tsp of cinnamon
1/4 tsp of nutmeg
1/4 tsp of cloves
Bread crumbs
2 Tbsp. of lemon juice

Method: Fill butter baking dish with alternate layers of raisons, apples and bread crumbs. Sprinkle each layer with combined dry ingredients. Dot with butter. Add lemon juice and water together and pour over mixtures. Cover and bake at 375-degree F for 45 minutes

Makes 8 servings

                        Serve warm

Stewed Raisons

1 cup of raisons
1 cup of water
1 Tbsp. of sugar

Method: Wash raisons, add water, cover and simmer 10 minutes. Add sugar, mix well and let simmer covered for 5 more minutes.

A very healthy, tasty treat.

Vickie Owens

Baked Apples

6 tart apples
6 Tbsp. of sugar
1 Tbsp. of butter
1/2 tsp of nutmeg
1/4 tsp of cinnamon

Method: Choose 6 medium apples, wash, remove stems and core. Cut a strip of skin from the upper portion of apples. Place in a baking dish. Combine sugar, nutmeg, and cinnamon and sprinkle inside apples. Dot each apple with butter. Pour 1/2 cup of water around apples and bake slowly at 325-degree F for 2-3 hours. You may also fill apples with diced marshmallows and chopped nuts.

Makes 6 servings

Apples smell delicious while baking
A nice healthy treat

Fried Apples

6 apples sliced and peeled

Hot grease

Method: Fry apples in hot grease for about 3 minutes.

Sprinkle lightly with cinnamon or sugar
An apple a day keeps the doctor away

Apple Crisp

6 cups of peeled and sliced apples
1 cup of uncooked oatmeal
1/2 cup of brown sugar
1/2 cup of melted butter
1/2 cup of flour

Method: Preheat oven to 375-degree F. Put sliced apples in an 8" sprayed square baking dish. Combine rest of ingredients, mix well until crumbly. Sprinkle this ingredient over apples. Bake 35-40 minutes until apples are tender.

Serves 8

Very good served warm with a scoop of
vanilla ice cream over the top

Apple Butter

6 cups of applesauce
2 cups of sugar
5 Tbsp. of cinnamon
3 Tbsp. of cider vinegar

Method: Mix all ingredients together in roasting pan and bake at 375-degree F. Make sure the lid is on the roasting pan. Stir once in a while until desired thickness. Once it reaches the desired thickness, let cool, place in lidded jars and keep in refrigerator.

Apple butter is delicious on warm homemade bread right out of the oven.

Very good on pancakes

Baked Custard

1 1/2 cups of milk
3 eggs, beaten
1/3 cup of sugar
1 tsp of vanilla
Cinnamon to taste

Method: Combine milk, eggs, sugar and vanilla. Beat until well combined. Pour into (4) 6 oz. custard cups or into a baking dish. Bake at 325-degree F for 30-45 minutes for 6 oz. cups or 50-60 minutes for baking dish.

This is good served warm or cold

Rice Pudding Made Simple

1/2 cup of uncooked rice
3 cups of boiling water
1/2 tsp of salt
1/2 cup of raisons
1/4 cup of butter or margarine
1 15 oz. can of sweet and condensed milk

Method: Cook rice, salt and water in double boiler about 40 minutes or until rice is tender. Stir in milk, butter, and raisons. Cook about 20 more minutes or until thick. Remove from heat, add vanilla and stir.

Serves about 8

A great after dinner dessert

Grape Nuts Pudding

1 cup of Grape Nuts
1 cup of raisons
1/2 cup of sugar
2 cups of water
1 small pkg. of lemon jello

Method: Boil Grape Nuts, raisons, sugar and water. Pour over lemon jello, not prepared. Stir until jello is dissolved.

Cool and serve with whipped cream

Peachy Delight

1 box of yellow cake mix
1 3/4 sticks of butter or margarine
1 large can of peaches, drained
1 pint of sour cream
3 egg yolks
Cinnamon to taste

Method: Combine yellow cake mix and butter. Press into a lightly greased 9x12" cake pan. Arrange peaches on top of this crust. Beat sour cream and egg yolks and pour over peaches, spreading evenly to the sides of the pan. Bake at 350-degree F for 20-30 minutes.

This peachy delight is very good served hot or cold

Put a bit of cool whip on top for a flavorful dessert

Vickie Owens

Easy Does It Peach Crunch

2 large cans of sliced peaches
Drain, but only remove 3/4 of the peach juice

1 box of Butter Brickle cake mix
1 stick of butter, melted

Method: Pour peaches and 3/4 of juice into a 9X13" cake pan light greased. Sprinkle half the Butter Brickle cake mix over the peaches. Drizzle with melted butter. Sprinkle the rest of the cake mix over the top. Bake at 350-degree F for 25-30 minutes.

Serve warm with vanilla ice cream
or a whipped topping

Peanut Butter Banana Dessert

1 slice of bread
Peanut butter
Thinly sliced banana
Honey

Method: Spread peanut butter generously on your slice of bread, top with sliced bananas and drizzle with honey.

This is a great breakfast treat for those in a hurry

A satisfying and nutritional treat for kids

Vickie Owens

Strawberry Banana Delight

Strawberries
Sugar to taste
Bananas

Method: As many strawberries as needed, mashed and sweetened with sugar to taste and topped with sliced bananas.

Pop in the blender and add a bit of milk and make yourself a strawberry-banana drink

Strawberry Banana Favorite

1 pt. of strawberries
3 to 4 bananas, sliced
10-12 grapes
4 pieces of bread

Method: Take half of the pint of strawberries and mash until juicy. Set aside.

Slice bananas

Tear a slice of bread in large crumb size pieces and place in a bowl. Add bananas, grapes and sliced strawberries. Toss.

Cover with mashed strawberry juice and top with whipped cream

Vickie Owens

Cheese Tart Delights

1-8 oz. pkg. of cream cheese
2 eggs
3/4 cup of sugar
1 Tbsp. of lemon juice
1 tsp of vanilla
Vanilla wafers
Fruit pie filling in the can

Method: Combine cream cheese, eggs, sugar, lemon juice and vanilla. Crush vanilla wafers and put 1-2 Tbsp. of wafer in the bottom of muffin cups. Spoon cream cheese mixture over wafers filling paper cups about 2/3 full. Bake at 350-degree F for 20 minutes. Cool. Remove paper muffins from tray, make a dent in muffin and fill with fruit pie filling, place back in oven on tray for about 2-3 minutes, just long enough to warm the filling.

Serves 24

					Delicious warm

Grandma's Date Roll

1 heaping Tbsp. of butter
2 cups of sugar
1/2 cup of milk
2 Tbsp. of white corn syrup
Pinch of salt
1 cup of dates, chopped
1 cup of black walnuts, chopped

Method: Boil sugar, butter, syrup, milk, and salt into the soft ball stage.

Pour on to a long sheet of waxed paper, cover with dates and walnuts, and shape into a roll. Wrap and let cool in refrigerator about 1 hour.

When cool slice and serve

                        Very tasty, easy dessert

Vickie Owens

Sugar Bread

1 slice of bread
Butter
Sugar

Method: Butter a slice of bread, cover with sugar and dust off loose granules.

Nothing else in the house to snack on have a piece of sugar bread.

This is what the Davis kids took to school in their lard can lunch pails. They had a slice of Grandma's homemade bread, spread with lard, tossed in sugar with a piece of fruit. Their lunch for the day.

It was handed down to my generation by my mom, only we substituted butter for lard and sprinkled it with sugar.

Christmas Crumble

3/4 lb. of vanilla wafers
1 cup of sugar
2 eggs
1 cup of crushed pineapple, drained
1/2 jar of maraschino cherries, drained
3/4 cup of chopped walnuts
1/2 cup of butter
1 quart of vanilla ice cream

Method: Crush vanilla wafers and spread half the crumbs on the bottom of a 9x13" cake pan. Cream sugar, butter and eggs together and spread over the crumbs in cake pan. Put in freezer until hard. Beat ice cream until soft, add walnuts, pineapple and cherries. Spread over frozen crumb layer. Return to freezer until hard and ready to serve.

Fresh Cow Pies

2 cups of milk
1 Bag of Chocolate chips
1 Tbsp. of shortening
1/2 cup raisons
1/2 cup of slivered almonds, chopped

Method: In double boiler over simmering water, melt milk chocolate chips and shortening. Stir until smooth. Remove from heat, mix in raisons and almond slivers. Drop by spoonful on waxed paper. Chill and serve.

Makes about 2 dozen.

Grandma's Divinity

3 cups of sugar
1/2 cup light corn syrup
1/2 cup of cold water
2 egg whites
1 tsp of vanilla

Method: Place sugar, water and syrup in pan over low heat. Stir only until sugar is dissolved; cook until it forms a soft ball in water. Beat egg whites until stiff. Continue beating egg whites until syrup mixture forms a hard ball and cracks when hit against the side of a cup. Add this syrup to stiffened egg whites, along with 1 tsp of vanilla. Continue to beat until thick enough to drop from a spoon.

Place by spoonsful on buttered pan. Nut meats can also be added just before ready to spoon. You can also add food coloring for the holiday seasons.

It is a very sweet treat

Vickie Owens

Grandpa's Butterscotch Treat

8 Tbsp. of butter
1 cup of sugar
1 Tbsp. of white syrup
1 Tbsp. of vinegar
2 Tbsp. of boiling water

Method: Boil all ingredients until you reach a ball stage. Pour into a jelly roll pan to cool down. Butter your hands and start pulling candy into little balls, and place on wax paper.

This candy can be time consuming so it wasn't made very often. Grandma made it in the winter when she was not able to get outside much because of the harsh winter months in the hill country.

This gave grandma something to do
during those cold winter months

Strawberry Divinity Fudge

2 cups of sugar
1/2 cup of water
1/4 tsp of cream of tartar
1 cup of preserved strawberries
2 egg whites

Method: Boil water, sugar and cream of tartar to form firm ball stage (248-degree F). Add strawberries that have been drained and dry as possible. Let this come to a boil. Pour slowly beating constantly over already stiffly beaten egg whites. Beat until thick and fluffy. Pour into well buttered pans.

When firm cut into squares

                    Makes lovely holiday candy

Carrot Fudge

1 1/2 cups of grated carrots
1/2 tsp of lemon flavoring
3 1/2 cups of sugar
1/2 cup of sweetened condensed milk

Method: Cook carrots, sugar and milk to ball stage. (234-238-degree F) Remove from stove and cool to room temperature. Beat until creamy. Pour into a buttered pan. Pat down with hands to 1" thickness

When firm cut into squares.

Makes about 2 dozen squares depending on the size of squares cut.

Another great treat for holidays

Pecan Treats

1 cup of light corn syrup
1 cup of sugar
1/2 lb. of pecans
5 Tbsp. of water
1 Tbsp. of butter

Method: Combine sugar, water, butter and corn syrup and bring to a rapid boil. Add pecans at rapid boil stage, stirring constantly. Mixture will form large bubbles on top and look sugary. Remove from heat and drop by spoonsful onto well buttered platter.

Delicious treat any time of the year

Vickie Owens

Molasses Squares

1/2 cup of sugar
1/3 cup of butter
1/3 cup of molasses
1/3 cup of water
Pinch of salt

Method: Combine all ingredients and bring to soft stage boil (275-280-degree F). Pour into a well buttered shallow pan. Let cool.

Cut into squares when cooled well.

Soda Cracker Sweets

Soda crackers
1 cup of brown sugar
1 cup of butter
1 12 oz. pkg. of chocolate chips

Method: Place soda crackers on the bottom of a foil lined buttered 10x15" cookie sheet

Boil sugar and butter to rolling boil for 3 minutes. Pour over crackers. Place in oven at 375-degree F for 5 minutes. Remove from oven and sprinkle chocolate chips over the top, return to oven for about 2-3 minutes. Spread melted chocolate chips evenly with spatula over crackers.

Refrigerate

Break into pieces and serve when cold

Hoarhound Candy

2 cups of hoarhound leaves, chopped
2 cups of boiling water
1/3 cup of white corn syrup
2 cups of sugar
1/8 tsp of salt

Method: Pour boiling water over Hoarhound. Allow to stand for 10 minutes.

Combine sugar, salt, corn syrup, and water from Hoarhound. Boil to soft crack stage (275-280-degree F).

Pour into a thin well buttered baking sheet. Mark into squares before candy hardens.

When hardened break off at marked squares and enjoy

Hoarhound can be very bitter; you may have to add extra sugar

Also good for coughs and cold medicine

Gooseberry Jelly

3 lbs. of green gooseberries
Sugar
Water

Method: Clean gooseberries in cold water and remove stem and blossoms.

Cover with water, cook slowly until soft. Drain through jelly bag. Combine sugar and gooseberry juice in equal proportions. Boil rapidly until jelly sheets form on spoon and pour into sterilized jars.

Gooseberry jelly is great on homemade bread
or on hot pancakes

Corn Meal Turnovers

1 1/2 cups of flour
3/4 cup of corn meal
2 Tbsp. of melted lard
1 egg, well beaten
1/2 tsp of salt
1/4 tsp of baking soda
2 tsp of baking powder
1 Tbsp. of sugar
1/2 cup of sour milk

Method: Sift flour, sugar, salt, baking soda, and baking powder. Add corn meal. Combine with eggs, lard and milk. Turn on lightly floured board. Pat into well oiled baking sheet pan 1/2" thick. Bake at 450-degree F for 8-10 minutes. When out of oven brush tops with melted butter, sprinkle with sugar and cinnamon and cut into square treats.

Homemade Cake Donuts

1 cup of sugar
4 tsp of baking powder
1 1/2 tsp of salt
1/2 tsp of nutmeg
2 eggs
1/4 cup of butter, melted
1 cup of milk
4 cups of flour
Oil for frying
Cinnamon and sugar to taste

Method: In a large bowl mix sugar, baking powder, salt and nutmeg. Add eggs, milk and melted butter and beat well. Add 3 cups of flour and beat well and then add the 4th cup of flour. Dough should be sticky. Refrigerate for 1 hour. Work half the dough at a time on floured board. If dough is still sticky add a little flour. Roll out., use glass or donut cutter to cut donuts, with a smaller hole in center. Dip in hot grease (360-degree F) and let cook 2-3 minutes, take out of oil and let dry on paper towel. Sprinkle with cinnamon and sugar mixture on sprinkle with powdered sugar.

Vickie Owens

FRED & ELLEN PHELP'S RECIPES

Vickie Owens

Corn Meal Mush

4 cups of water, divided
1 cup of corn meal
1 tsp of salt
Oil for frying
Syrup

Method: Boil 3 cups of water with corn meal and salt. Add to remaining boiling water. Stir until mixture comes to a boil. Reduce heat, cover and simmer for 1 hour; stirring occasionally. Pour in to a greased 8x4" loaf pan. Chill 8 hours or overnight. Cut into 1/2" slices and fry in oil. Cover with warm syrup and eat.

A great breakfast meal to be made the night before

Easy Pickles

1 cup of sugar
1 cup of vinegar
1 tsp of salt

Boil these three ingredients together for 3 minutes.

Add
1/2 tsp mustard seed
1/4 tsp of celery seed
1/4 Tbsp. of turmeric

Fill a pint jar with fresh sliced cucumbers and sliced onions. Pour the hot syrup over the cucumbers and onions, seal lid on jar

These will keep in refrigerate for a long time

You may also add diced green pepper to the pickles

Sunshine Dill Pickles

In a gallon jar, put 1-2 hands full of dill in the bottom of the jar. Fill with large and small cucumbers. Add 3-4 cloves of garlic, plus 6 tablespoons of canning salt. On top of cucumbers and garlic, lay a piece of rye bread. Fill with jar with warm water and loosely seal and set in the sun for 3-4 days. Then, throw away the bread.

Refrigerate and enjoy!

NOTE: You can use 1/4 tsp. of garlic powder in place of the clove of garlic if you like

Green Tomato Mincemeat

13 pounds of green tomatoes
1 quart sliced fresh apples
1 pound raisons
1 pound chopped suet
2 1/2 lbs. brown sugar
3 sliced lemons
cinnamon, cloves and nutmeg to taste

Method: Wash tomatoes and cut or grind into small pieces. Sprinkle with salt. Let stand overnight. Drain. Add water to prevent sticking. Cook 30 minutes. Add lemon juice and grated rind of one lemon and the white pare of another lemon, which is cut into small pieces. Add apples, suet, raisins and a few grains of salt. Simmer slowly, stirring frequently until the apples and tomatoes are tender and the flavor is blended. Pack in sterilized jars and seal.

Tomato Jam

Mix equal amounts of sugar and tomato pulp. Let stand for 2 hours. (6 cups of pulp is recommended). Add 1/2 lemon and cook for 10 minutes. Add 1 box of sure jell and cook 3 more minutes. Seal in sterilized jars.

Apple Butter

2 gallons sliced apples (not pealed)
10 cups of sugar
Let stand overnight.
Add 1 tablespoon cinnamon, 2 tablespoons red hot candies and put into a kettle with a tight lid. Cook 2 hours. (DO NOT PEEK) Rub through a sieve and can in sterilized jars.

Ground Cherry Preserves

4 Cups cooked ground cherries
4 cups sugar
1 lemon, finely sliced
Cook slowly for 20 minutes or until the lemon is well cooked.
Ready to serve on homemade bread.

Rhubarb Jam

3 cups rhubarb
1/2 cup water (NOTE: Use less water when rhubarb is very moist).
Add 2 1/2 cups sugar
Bring to a boil and add 1 small box of strawberry jello

This can be jarred and stored in refrigerator

Vickie Owens

Apple Crisp

8 cups sliced apples -- you can leave some of the skins on
1 1/2 cups brown sugar
1 1/2 cups flour
1 c. butter or margarine
2 cups oatmeal
A dash or cinnamon
Sprinkle the cinnamon over the apples
Bake for 40 minutes at 350 degrees F in a 9" by 13" glass baking dish.

Rhubarb Crisp

1 cup of sugar
1 cup of flour
2 tsp baking powder
2 Tbsp. of shortening
3\4 cup of milk
Dash of salt
Mix all above ingredients together and put into a 9x13" glass baking dish. Put 4 or 5 cut up cups of rhubarb on top. Pour 1 cup sugar and 1 cup of hot water on top. Bake at 400 degrees F for 35 minutes

Glorified Rice

1 package lemon jello
1 cup of cooked rice
About 3/4 container of Cool-Whip or 1 cup real whipped cream
15 oz. can crush pineapple, drained
12-15 mini marshmallows
When the jello is set, fold in other ingredients

Thank You

Fred and Ellen Phelps for the lovely recipes

Vickie Owens

Granddaughter of Lillian Ann (Cole) Davis and Charley Davis

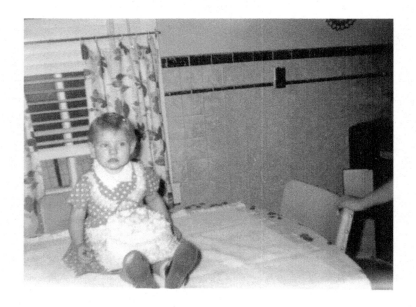

Vickie Owens Poetry

Our Sunday Stroll

Remembering when, so long ago,
We'd take that trip, our Sunday stroll,
Twenty-six miles we traveled afar,
Couldn't wait to get to Grandma & Grandpa's
Out of that car!
Reaching our destiny, we still have the path,
Three quarters of a mile in woods deep,
Birds chirping, bunnies running,
Flowers blooming, smell so sweet,
Whispering winds some Sunday's howl,
Clouds overcast may bring a scowl.
Are we there yet?
Another bend in the wind,
The sweet aroma of the cabin is coming near,
Homemade bread and gooseberry pie,
Grandma has baked us a treat,
I know when the opening to the cabin is near,
I feel it, smell it, aromas everywhere,
And there it is,
Full of life and good cheer,
All because Grandma and Grandpa live here.

The Long and Winding Path

The winding path pitch dark at night,
Wish there was a moon,
To guide me by its light,
There is not, I shall walk in fear,
The woods are asleep,
But yet what do I hear?
Crackling branches under my feet,
Coyotes howl, owls saying, "Who,"
Rustling of bushes,
I await the moon to shine through,
I stop dead in the path,
Lighting matches as I go,
Trying to find my way in the darkened glow,
I hear a rumble as I tip toe,
It's the four-wheeler, headlights bright,
I can now see in the dark of night,
Scared out of my wits,
I shall not let it show,
I am the brave one,
Don't you know.

Vickie Owens

Grandma

Grandma is a woman I remember,
With long white silky hair,
All wrapped up in a bun,
We use to brush it, 100 strokes,
Just for fun,
Her flour sack apron
Hung over the length of her dress,
She didn't have anyone to impress,
A cane in one hand,
A five-gallon bucket in the other,
Off to the woods she would go,
To see what she could discover.
A few black snakes
Waiting to be tossed out of her way,
With the cane she used for hunting prey,
Scratched up arms and forearms,
She was enjoying what she loved to do,
Picking blackberries and gooseberries,
Until there was no more,
She came out of the woods; picked and cleaned,
Tossed them in a pie,
A delicious dessert before we had to say
Goodbye.

Grandpa

Grandpa brings back memories so fine,
A tall stern man with no defeat,
A buck saw and ax was his way,
To build the Old Log Cabin,
Back in the day,
Using his gun to hunt prey,
For food filled days,
Living off the land nestled deep in the woods,
Raising nine children the best he could,
This was his haven for years to pass,
Plowing and cropping,
He made it last,
A chew of tobacco,
Late nights,
A string of his guitar,
A song sung,
Under the Northern star.
A peaceful way to end his day.

The Children

There once were nine children
living deep in the woods,
In a log cabin filled with goods,
They'd walk to school with lard can in hand,
Trying to learn the best they can,
Finishing their school day,
Come home, do chores and hunt prey,
This is how they filled their day,
Night time would fall,
It was their call,
To hustle the wooden stairs,
Climb in their feather ticks for the night,
Snuggle up tight, the North wind does bite,
Seeping through the cracks in the windows,
Not sealed very tight,
Through all of this it is no wonder,
They lost their sister to the fight,
Of catching pneumonia through the night,
So now there are eight instead of nine,
This made things a bit unkind,
They never gave up the fight,
To be a family of eight, deep in the woods,
Every day and every night.

Whispering Pine

Whispering pine, I sit high upon the brae,
Looking down into the valley,
At the harsh grown hay,
Thinking back to yesterday,
If only for a second I treasure this time,
Of deep thought among the vine,
I once was a child running wild and free,
Listening to the bluebirds sing softly to me,
Now that I've aged,
With no reason or rhyme,
Nothing seems the same,
As it did back in time,
Sitting among
The Whispering Pine

Deep in The Valley

Deep in the valley,
Where the tall grass grows,
I find bees and flowers,
Birds galore,
Dandelions wild and free,
Rabbits running rambunctiously,
Sunshine enlightening my day,
I walk barefoot,
Grass tickles between my toes,
Honeysuckles sweet to my nose,
This really is the valley,
Where few seldom go,
It is deep and profound,
Sustainable and alive,
This is how nature thrives,
With only me amongst it all.
Might this be my call?
Is it here I belong?
In the most beautiful valley of all.

Changes Over Time

Like the seasons and the trees,
An Autumn breeze,
Colors of gold and bronze,
Crispness in the air,
I walk freely,
Without a care,
Leaves rustle below my feet,
My life in a constant state of change,
More beautiful as I age,
Turning the colors of time,
Only seasons,
Frame my mind.

Summer's Dream

The sea shines the shore,
Where pebbled sand lay,
In just a glimpse,
I see children at play,
Sandy beach,
Sunlight's ray,
Soft bronzed skin,
Sailboats skyward,
In the wind,
Summer's dream,
Lest they be,
It is me,
Who walks the shores by the sea.

Spring's Awakening

Spring is the time of year,
You get a fever,
One that can be cured,
Spring enlightens your heart,
Makes you feel free,
Enjoying the buds and blossoms on the trees,
The smell of fresh daisies and lilacs,
Bluebirds singing to me,
What better way to wake up my day,
Full of sunshine,
Beautiful flowers aglow,
Buzzing with bees to make them grow,
Soft green grass, I shall walk the path,
In the warm heat of the day,
It's okay,
Bring spring showers in May.

Vickie Owens

Autumn is Near

Autumn is the grandest season of all,
There is a coldness to the air,
The leaves on the trees are changing,
Colors are brilliant and bold,
They fall upon the ground one by one,
Harvest days coming to an end,
Fields are getting bare,
But yet the hillsides are ablaze,
With the beauty of its leaves,
Some are still not blown from the trees,
As I stare,
Wrapped in my sweater wear,
A gentle reminder,
To enjoy what days are left of fall,
It won't be long
And winter will give its call.

Winter Upon Us

Winter brings the bitterly cold,
Warmed by the wood,
Of a fireplace burning,
A glass of wine as we dine,
Snuggled in quilts to keep us warm,
Enjoy baking during a winter storm,
Snowflakes fall,
Children ice skating without a care,
Piled up snow everywhere,
The sound of graters going past,
Does this mean the storm will last?
For a day… maybe a week,
Off to shovel, before the next peak,
The cold winter months are upon us all,
Stay snuggled and warm,
Watch the snowflakes fall,
For it won't be long now,
Holiday will be here,
Christmas,
A joyous time of the year,
May it bring you good cheer.

Vickie Owens

Mom and Dad

Mom and Dad gave birth to me,
Fifty-nine years ago,
Brought me into this world,
Not knowing how far I would go,
The roads I would travel,
The distance,
Or how my life would be,
They are gone now,
They passed on without me,
They left me all alone,
To guide myself in the right way,
They would be proud of all my accomplishments,
If only they could see me today,
The struggles I've been through,
The children that I have raised,
The woman I have become,
Never giving up along the way,
It is them that gave me the strength,
To be my own unique person today.

Family Ties

There is none better than to know,
You have family that love you,
But...Sometimes this is not true,
For your family drifts away,
Once parents decease,
The bond is no longer there,
Sadness and such despair,
Feeling lost with nowhere to go,
Memories are what you hold,
Brothers and sisters who once made you laugh,
And sometimes cry,
Can only be found in pictures,
Memories to cherish,
This brings comfort, no despair,
But to think…
There was a time, your family was there,
To love and laugh,
And truly care.

Vickie Owens

No Love Gained

My broken heart weeps,
For what you have done,
I fell in love with a shining son,
Little did I know it would be shortened so,
I would sit alone this day,
My cries you will hear,
Yet I stay strong,
Proud of who I am,
My world will go on,
With no sorrow,
But yes, there is pain,
Of no love gained.

Love Gone Away

Alas you come to me,
With words spoken from your mind,
Making me wonder what happened,
In all the days that were so kind,
The cherished moments shared,
Miles traveled along the way,
Only to find,
My love I gave away, was never meant to stay,
The shortened miles are longer now,
The cherished moments are few today,
I've been told it is not his time,
To give his heart away.
For his words I shall treasure,
Respect his thoughts,
As gracefully as I may,
Praying he will find his True Love someday.

Vickie Owens

Rainy Days

As tears fall, it begins to rain,
Pecking at my window pane,
Lost,
With nowhere to go,
Gloomy days have their way to show,
Waiting for sunshine to ease the pain,
Of dear ones lost with no regain,
Am I mourning for those I love?
Or remembering the past?
Here today,
And then we go,
To a better place where no one knows,
The sun will shine, bring brighter days,
Time to remember,
The fun filled ways,
Rain if you may,
Mourn if I will,
No more rain,
To make things still.

Lavender Scented Candle Light

As I sit here tonight,
I write by lavender scented candle light,
The soft glow glistens my room,
Feeling much comfort,
Deep within my womb,
Peace comes to mind, love in my heart,
For those who surround me,
And played such a big part,
Life has never been easy,
A struggle along the way,
Experiences I wished would never stay,
Love that has come and drifted afar,
Why did it leave such a scar?
Angels come from heaven above,
Guided my life to forgiveness and love,
I now pray for those who are bewildered and sad,
Life is one of the greatest gifts we have,
Don't be afraid to reach out,
Touch the ones you love, family and friends,
And the good Lord above,
Now that I have found peace for the night,
I will blow out
My Lavender Scented Candle Light.

Skin Like Iron

She wears her skin like iron,
Yet still soft from within,
Tears trickle down her weathered facial skin,
Growing old is a final glimpse,
Of who she might not want to be,
A thousand miles from nowhere,
Time makes no matter to thee,
The rebel has vanished,
The strength is gone,
The mind lives on,
Clever as it can be,
A reminder, it is never too late,
To fulfill dreams,
That will set her free.

Weathered Roots

The Life They Built Together

Vickie Owens

PICTURES

Vickie Owens

Grandma-Lillian Ann (Cole) Davis

Jan 26, 1894-Sept 16, 1962

Grandma sits relaxing after a hard day's work

This picture shows grandma at her sister's house (Alta Bolsinger) in Graham, Iowa. She is showing off her five buckle boots. I am certain she and Alta will soon be in the woods picking blackberries and gooseberries.

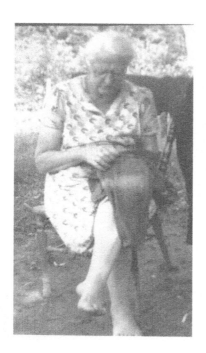

Grandma is sitting, but her work still is not done. She is mending pants for someone.

Grandma loved her two dogs, Trix and Rex

Grandma Davis with grandson, Gary Ostrander, son of Mary and Clarence Ostrander. Picture taken in Spring of 1962

Grandma, (Lillian Davis) with grandchildren and great-grandchildren. Left to right, Vickie Ostrander Owens, Lee (Tom) Ostrander,
Sitting on Grandma's lap, Douglas (Casey) Cardy. son of Phyllis Ostrander Cardy, Patty Davis, daughter of Clarence (Gink) Davis, is holding Jeff Cardy also the son of Phyllis Ostrander Cardy.

Grandma and daughter, Minnie

Minnie is now 91 years old and is the last living child of Charley and Lillian Davis.

She has proven to be a strong Pioneer Woman

Minnie now resides at:
Stonehill Community Care Center
in
Dubuque, Iowa

Grandma (Lillian Ann Cole Davis)

With

Daughter-In-Law (Lorraine Goerdt Davis)

Wife of son, Clarence (Gink) Davis

**Lillian Ann Cole Davis
Passed away on September 16, 1962.**

Vickie Owens

Grandpa-Charley Davis

March 7, 1887-August 8, 1975

Vickie Owens

Grandpa Davis did not like his picture taken, so there will not be many pictures of him. Here he enjoys some free time and sunshine on his ten acres. Behind him are boards laid out with walnuts drying in the sun.

Grandpa sits beside the old wooden table in the kitchen at The Old Log Cabin.

Grandpa Davis stands tall and stern. This picture was taken while living with his daughter, Mary A. Ostrander at 384 Southern Ave., Dubuque, Iowa. He begrudgingly agreed to this picture.

Grandpa
(Charley Davis)

Grandpa enjoying his day with some of his Great-Grandchildren
Left to Right: Jim Klossner Randy Meyer, Merle Klossner, Ronnie Klossner, Penny Klossner, & Madge Klossner

Grandpa
(Charley Davis)
Celebrating his
85th Birthday at
his daughter's house.
(Mary Ostrander), this is
where Charley resided for
many years.

Grandpa, (Charley Davis)
is being visited by three of
his daughters.
Left to Right:
Minnie Davis Ward
Fannie Davis Wardle
Mary Davis Ostrander

Vickie Owens

Grandpa (Charley Davis) is being visited by his son Merle James "Jim" Davis and his great –grandson, Jason Heth, who now practices medicine:
Dr. Jason Heth, MD., Neurosurgery,
Ann Arbor, Michigan

Vickie Owens

Charley and Lillian's Log Cabin Kids

Vickie Owens

The Children
Of
Charley and Lillian Davis

From the top of the tree left to right

Fannie Davis Wardle

Merle "Jim" Davis

Mary Davis Ostrander

Charley and Lillian Davis

Roy "Dew Drop" Davis

Clarence "Gink" Davis

Minnie "Sook" Davis Ward

Dorothy Davis (deceased at the age of 3)

Cletus "Clete" Davis

Virginia "Sis" Davis Donath

Charley and Lillian's Log Cabin Kids

Vickie Owens

MISCELLANEOUS FAMILY PICTURES
NEWSPAPER CLIPPINGS
SHORT STORIES

Vickie Owens

Mary Ann Angel Cole Livingston

Mother of Lillian Ann Cole Davis

Mary Ann Angel married John Cole, who is buried at Oak Hill Cemetery. Mary Ann was born in Ohio and was the daughter of John Angel and Sarah Waymer. On January 30, 1912, three years after John's death, Mary Ann married Eli Livington. In 1924 Mary Ann divorced Eli and went to live with her two sons, 4 miles East of Colesburg, IA. In the year 1925 when the Little Turkey River flooded, Mary was washed from her home and drown. It is said that the Little Turkey had not risen that high in 80 years.

Vickie Owens

WARNING

Mary was warned of the flood, but refused to leave her home. It is said her body was later found in the Little Turkey River with her hair entangled in river branches near Millville, Iowa. Attached are some newspaper clippings of her drowning.

HUNT FOR BODY OF WOMAN THOUGHT VICTIM OF STORM

Manchester, Ia., June 17.—(By the Associated Press.)—Searchers still are continuing to hunt for the body of Mrs. Mary Cole of Colesburg, who was drowned near her home early Monday, but no trace of it has been found. Reports that she had been found alive are denied at Colesburg.

Chalker Rippon, who was injured at noon yesterday by a cavein on the Illinois Central bridge, died in the afternoon. A. A. Reedy, who was injured at the same time is still alive but little hopes are held out for his recovery.

SELECT PRENTER

Mrs. Mary Livingston, more than 60 yrs. old was drowned in the flood of little Turkey Creek, about eleven miles from Guttenberg, early Monday morning. Her home was completely destroyed by the force of the waters. Barns and other buildings with live stock were also carried down the stream. Mrs. Livingston and Bob and Joe Cole, 2 sons by her previous marriage were aroused by the storm Sunday night. It is said that Joe suggested for them to swim to a higher point for safety which he did, while the mother and his brother Bob not realizing the danger of the flood remained in the house. The house finally was dashed into pieces. Bob saved himself by staying in a tree all night, while his mother was swept down the stream. She was found yesterday afternoon by Mr. Reinitz and Mr. Andregg at Kauffman's Bottom near Millville. Her clothing and furniture had been seen down stream. It is said that he water in Little Turkey Creek has not been as high in 50 years.

Obituary

Mrs. Mary Angel Cole was born in Ohio on August 26, 1858, and drown on June 15, 1925 at the age of 66 years, 9 months and 19 days old.

Her husband, John Cole preceded her in death several years earlier. The following children survive: Fred, James, Bert, Joseph, Michael and Robert Cole, Mrs. Sarah "Sadie" Yonkovic, Mrs. Myrtle Pierce, Mrs. Alta Bolsinger, and Mrs. Lillian Davis, also a number of grandchildren and many other relatives and friends.

Funeral service will be held Friday, at the M. E. Church, officiated by Rev W. H. Smith. Interment was made at Oak Hill Cemetery, Colesburg, IA. Sympathy is extended to the family in the sad death of their loved one.

Mary Ann Angel Cole has no grave marker at this time. She is laid to rest at Oakhill Cemetery in Colesburg, IA.

Her husband John Cole is buried in Oakhill Cemetery, Colesburg, IA.

John Cole

Husband of Mary Ann Angel Cole

Father of Lillian Ann Cole Davis

May 2, 1857-August 15, 1909

Died at the age of 53 from blood poisoning

Children of Mary Angel Cole and John Cole

Alta Bolsinger   James Cole

Lillian Cole Davis   Fred Cole

Sarah E. Yonkovic   Bert Cole

Myrtle Cole Pirc

Michael Henry "Mike" Cole-No Headstone

Father of Charley Davis

Charles B. J. Davis

March 21, 1844-May 2, 1902

Vickie Owens

Charles B. J. Davis
Father of Charley Davis

Charles B. J. Davis was born March 21, 1844 in Newport County, Rhode Island. He passed away at his home in Colesburg, IA on May 2, 1902. He married Alice Chambers on Oct. 11, 1868. They married in Cassville, WI. They had ten children. Charles was a Civil War Veteran serving in Co. A, 45th Illinois Volunteer Infantry. He enlisted as a private for a period of one year. He was mustered out on July 12, 1865 in Louisville, Kentucky. His occupation was a farmer in Colesburg, IA.

Charles B.J. Davis and Alice (Chambers) Davis are laid to rest in Oakhill Cemetery, Colesburg, Iowa.

Alice Chambers Davis, wife, was born July 1, 1849 in New York and died August 1, 1933 in Colesburg, IA.

Children of Charles B. J. Davis
and
Alice Chambers Davis

Martha Ann Davis Spores

Robert Davis   Charley Davis

David Davis   Edna Davis Harry

Children continued on next page

Weathered Roots

Mary Davis Parsons

Thomas Henry Davis

Perry Edward Davis

Nellie Davis Bolsinger

Earban Davis

Vickie Owens

**Captain Charles Button Davis Sr.
Grandfather of Charley Davis**

Born in Freetown, Bristol, Massachusetts
May 29, 1819-April 5, 1885

Married to Mary Barker Davis
December 11, 1818-April 13, 1893

Vickie Owens

**Charles Button Davis Sr.
Sea Captain of the Bark Julia Ann
San Francisco, California**

Vickie Owens

Sea Captain

Charles Button Davis was a seafaring man, but he died an Iowa farmer. He was born on 5/29/1819 in Freetown, Bristol, Massachusetts. In his youth he traveled the world by ship, horse and wheelbarrow. He came to his rest in Delaware, County, Iowa on April 5, 1885. Between those years his life touched many other lives.

Little is known about his early childhood years. At age 22 he received his Seaman Protective Certificate, around 1840. Later, he became ship's Captain of the Bark Julia Ann. The Julia Ann, a cargo ship, sailed from San Francisco, California to Australia and back. Captain Davis frequently carried human contraband; Mormons going on church missions and returning.

In 1853, Davis smuggled a famous political prisoner; John Mitchel, an Irish nationalist/revolutionist, lawyer, and political journalist from Australia. (P. J. Smyth, a journalist in New York, arranged to have Mitchel smuggled out of Australia). Other Irish prisoners were also smuggled out of Australia at that time.

Mitchel was taken by the boat *Emma* from Tasmania to Sydney, Australia. Once at Sydney, Mitchel met up with his family and they were put on the Julia Ann. **Captain Charles Button Davis** was the **Master** of the **Julia Ann** at that time and he brought the Mitchel family to the United States along with other Mormon passengers and cargo. Captain Davis's activities were scrutinized by the U.S. and Australian Governments. He was "advised" against further smuggling or he would go to prison.

He was captain of the Julia Ann until July of 1854, before the infamous wreck under Captain Pond, ship's owner, where five Mormons were lost at sea. The wreck of the Julia Ann can be seen on YouTube. It is believed once he left the Julia Ann he turned to *whaling* off the shores of Massachusetts; Whaling was a tough and dangerous job that sometimes kept Whalers out to sea for more than a year at a time.

The 1860 Census, Newport, Rhode Island, shows Charles B. Davis, 40, Mariner, Mary 42, and children Thomas Charles, Jr., Emeline, Orin F. and Edward.

Capt. Davis finally left the sea and headed for Iowa. It was told by great-granddaughter, Jane Gates Koeller how Captain Charles Davis put all of his belongings in a wheelbarrow, with Johnny cakes hanging from the handles and walked across the country.

Once established he sent for his family. In the 1870 Census, he is a farmer, at Colony, Delaware County, Iowa, and his wife Mary, and children: Charles Jr., Emeline, Orin and Edwin are with him. (NOTE: An entry of this same census and living next to Capt. and Mary Davis, is W.P.E. Barker, 50, farmer, born in R.I., Sarah 40, children: Ida, William, Jane, and Eva. I believe this is likely a brother to Mary Barker Davis, Capt. Charles Davis wife).

Captain Charles Davis purchased land in Delaware County, Iowa, and on Sept. 5, 1876 he sold it to John V. Bush, and he purchased other land and moved the family to Honey Creek, Delaware County, Iowa.

In 1969 Celeste Busby received a letter from Helen Gates Bolle, before her passing, that stated, "Captain Charles B. Davis left his mark all over the world." He would be worth researching further.

Charles Button Davis Sr.
Sea Captain on the Bark Julia Ann
San Francisco, California

A list of the Sea Captains who sailed ship during the 1800's can be found by doing a search of Sea Captains during the 1800's, on the internet in San Francisco, California. Captain Davis is listed on the Sea Captain list. This list shows he had an office at 18 Howard Street in San Francisco, California.

The owner of the Julia Ann, Captain Pond, who was the Sea Captain at the time of the wreck of the Julia Ann, which took five Mormon's lives can be viewed on YouTube. Search for *Divine Providence Final Cut.*

Captain Charles B. Davis
May 29, 1819-April 5, 1885

Captain Davis is laid to rest at
Thorpe Union Cemetery
Manchester, Iowa

Mary Barker Davis, Wife
December 11, 1818-April 13, 1893

Married Capt. Charles B. Davis
February 22, 1839

Mary Barker Davis is laid to rest at
Thorpe Union Cemetery
Manchester, Iowa

No headstone can be found

Vickie Owens

Children of Capt. Charles B Davis Sr. and Mary Barker Davis

Vickie Owens

Children

Thomas Davis	1840-?
Charles B. J. Davis	1844-1902
Maria Emeline Davis	1849-1901
Orin F. Davis	1854-1922
Edward Davis	1857-?

Emeline and Charles B J Davis were the only headstones for the children of Captain Charles B. Davis that could be found.

Vickie Owens

GENEALOGY
Davis-Cole
Three Generations

Vickie Owens

Charley Davis
B: 3/7/1887 D: 8/8/1975
Married: Lillian Ann Cole
5/30/1915

Lillian Ann
B: 1/26/1894 D: 9/16/1962
Laid to rest at Oakhill Cemetery
Colesburg, Iowa

Children

Fannie Davis Wardle-B: 8/22/1915 –D:9/9/1998
Spouse Howard Wardle-B: 6/5/1902-D:12/25/1982
Children: Charles-B:6/10/1939-D:11/8/1944, Beverly Wardle Steger B: 11/15/36-D: 11/5/2012, Roger Wardle, Judy Wardle, Janice Wardle, Kathy Wardle, Diane Wardle Brecht, Connie Wardle McIntyre

Merle James Davis-B 10/8/1917-D:5/3/1976
Spouse Leonora Gruber Davis-B 9/71923-D:12/20/1994
Children: Leona (Sandy) Davis Heth

Mary Alice Davis Ostrander-B: 6/13/1920-D:7/1/1994
Spouse Clarence E. Ostrander-B: 11/25/1917-D:8/9/1984
Children: Phyllis Ostrander Cardy, Jean Ostrander Klossner, Clarence A Ostrander, B: 11/3/1940 D: 9/25/1998,
Merle Ostrander, Robert Ostrander,
Diane Ostrander Meyer B: 6/28/1947 D: 8/14/2008,
Lee Ostrander, Charles Ostrander,
Vickie Ostrander Owens, Gary Ostrander

Roy Edward Davis B: 8/25/1922 D: 11/28/1998
Spouse: Neva Scott (divorced) Children: Chris Davis, Roy (Punk) Davis Jr. B: 10/8/1956 D: 8/3/2015, Gerald (Gary) Davis.

Dorothy Davis B: 4/14/1928 D: 11/20/1932

Cletus Davis B: 1/9/1932 D: 2/8/2016 Spouse: Mildred Hueneke, Children: Lonny Davis, Pamela Davis Gregorich, Julie Davis, Kevin Davis, Randy Davis.

Clarence E. Davis B: 8/13/1934 D: 11/25/2003
Spouse: Lorraine Goerdt B: 1/2/1930 D: 9/17/1973
Children: Clarence Davis, Patricia Davis, Donald Davis, Dale Davis.

Minnie Davis Ward B: 10/9/1925, Spouse: Donald F. Ward B: 3/21/1921 D: 11/7/1998 Children: Donald F. Ward Jr. B: 6/13/1943 D: 9/20/2004, Mary Ward B:(?) D: 4/17/1946, James J. Ward B:3/26/1947 D: 5/28/1947, Gloria Kramer, Ruby Otting, Cletus Ward, Richard Ward, B: 12/31/1953 D: 6/19/2006, John Ward, B: 7/11/1956 D: 5/18/2012, Ronald Ward, Phyllis Arensdorf, Gary Ward, B: 6/13/1961, D: 6/29/1977, Raymond Ward, Gail A. Huston

Virginia L. Davis Donath B: 11/3/1934 D: 12/6/2005
Spouse: Walter Donath (divorced) Children: Rick Donath, Jerry Donath, Walter Donath, Greg Donath, Brenda Donath Briggs. Owen Donath, B: 12/7/1961 D: 1/5/1995.

Charles B. J. Davis (Great Grandfather)
B: 3/21/1844 D: 5/2/1902

Married Alice Chambers
October 11, 1868
Alice Chambers
B: 7/1/1849 D: 8/1/1933

Children

Mary Davis Parsons, B:12/14/1869 D: 12/2/1919 Spouse: William Parsons B: Abt. 1861 D: 1924, Children: Jenny Parsons B; Abt. 1895 D: (?), Nellie Bolsinger B: 3/14/1901 D: 3/20/1927, Wesley Parsons B: 3/1/1904 D: 6/4/1972

Thomas H. Davis, B: 4/26/1871 D: 9/23/1940
Spouse: Etta Knickerbocker, B: 3/1885 D: 4/13/1905, Children: Jessie Davis B: 12/22/1894 D: 10/7/1918, Harry Davis, B: 1/15/1901 D: 8/13/1906 Spouse: Mary Sophia Kaufmann Davis, B: 4/26/1871 D: 9/23/1940 Children: Stella Kiernan B: 2/11/1908 D: 1/21/1978, Charles N. Davis B: 3/4/1910 D: 3/7/1969, Hazel Smothers, B: 2/24/1912 D: 3/29/1982, Ethel Carr B: 10/5/1913 D: 7/28/1974 Thomas R. Davis B: 2/13/1921 D: 4/14/1989, Bertha Phillips B: 11/10/1922 D: 8/24/2008, Edna Fishnick B: 4/17/1925 D: 9/12/1995, Walter W. Davis B: 9/24/1926 D: 3/8/2002, Carl Davis B: 11/22/1928 D: 10/25/1998, Albert E. Davis B: 5/26/1931 D: 7/25/2013

Perry E. Davis, B: 3/28/1876 D: 3/2/1934, Spouse: Martha J. Spores B: 10/25/1882 D: 9/1/1976, Children: Edith M. Davis, B: 10/1897, D: 4/8/1955, Norma Davis, B: Abt. 1900, D: unknown, Norman E. Davis, B: 5/20/1900 D: 10/25/1987, Arthur Davis, B: 11/8/1902 D: 7/1977, Irving Davis B: 1904, D: 1989 Della F.

Davis, B: 4/19/1906 D: 3/26/2004 Robert Davis, B: 1908 D: 2/1979, Ruth Davis, B: Abt. 1910, D: unknown, Floyd Davis, B: 3/19/1913, D: 12/15/1992, Odessa L. Davis, B: Abt. 1914, D: 1968, Roy E. Davis, B: 6/8/1917, D: 2/22/1989

Nellie Davis Bolsinger, B: 7/26/1878 D: 3/15/1933 Spouse: Charles Jeff Bolsinger B: 6/12/1873, D: 3/1946, Children: Alice Bolsinger, B: 8/2/1897, D: 5/3/1922, Daymond J. Bolsinger, B: 9/21/1898, D: 6/1971, Ada Bolsinger, B: 1901 (?) D: unknown,
Martha Bolsinger, B: 1907 (?) D: 1928, Clara Bolsinger, B:1905 D: 1911

Earban Davis, B: 7/10/1881, D: 1952, Spouse: Rose Knickerbocker, B: 7/12/1884 D: 12/23/1918, Children: Earnest Davis, B: Abt. 1907, D: 1975, Viola Davis, B: Abt. 1910, D: Unknown. 2nd Spouse: Rebecca A. Spores B: 9/3/1885 D: 1/11/1961, Children: Velma M. Curler B: 7/21/1901 D: 12/28/1918, Gertrude O. Kauffman, B: 10/22/1909, D: 8/20/1986, Ralph L. Davis, B: 6/27/1914 D: 4/14/1916, Bessie Hoisington,B: 8/30/1918 D: 6/10/1988

Martha Ann Davis Spores B: 5/17/1884 D: 10/23/1947 Spouse: James W. Spores B: 1/2/1879 D: 6/24/1976 Children: Lilian D. Spores B: Abt. 1903, D: Unknown, Audrey Spores, B: 1904 D: Unknown, Harold R. Spores, B: Abt. 1905 D: Unknown, James L. Spores, B: Abt. 1909 D: Unknown, Blanchie A. Spores, B: Abt. 1911, D: Unknown, Alfred Spores, B: Abt. 1915 D: Unknown, Alba Spores, B: Unknown D: Unknown, Spencer Spores, B: Abt. 1917 D: Unknown, Russell Spores B; Abt. 1919 D: Unknown

Charley Davis-All information about Charley Davis and family begins on page 325-326.

Robert I. Davis, B: 9/27/1889 D: 2/23/1956 Spouse: Mabel Chambers, B: 4/13/1899 D: 3/12/1961, Children: Louisa G. Davis B: 5/25/1915 D: 2/12/1987, Berdeno E. Davis B: 12/20/1916, D: 1/1979, Luther C. Davis, B: 12/9/1925, D: 11/7/2006

David Davis, B: 11/7/1891 D: 1952, Spouse: Velma Gretchen Curler, B: 11/19/1902 D: 3/4/1968. Children: Myrtle Bond, B: 8/9/1920 D: 5/1982, Genevieve G. Williams B: 4/1/1923 D: 4/21/2008

Edna Marie Davis, Harry, B: 3/27/1894 D: 8/17/1986 Spouse: James Cleveland Harry, B: 9/24/1884 D: 1/1969, Children: Donald Harry, B: 5/24/1920, D: 12/15/1932.

Vickie Owens

Capt. Charles Button Davis Sr.
(Great-Great Grandfather)
B: 5/29/1819 D: 4/5/1885

Married Mary Barker
February 22, 1839
Mary Barker
B: 12/11/1818 D: 4/13/1893

Children

Thomas Davis, B: 1840 D: Unknown Spouse: Mary Davis, B: Abt. 1841 D: Unknown, Children: Unknown at this time.

Charles B. J. Davis, information can be seen on page 327-328.

Maria Emeline Davis, B: 12/10/1849 D: 12/28/1901 Spouse: Rufus Rollin Gates, B: 7/27/1847 D: 8/1/1935, Children: Sylvia E. Gates, B: Abt. 1868 D: 3/1898, Winfield S. Gates, B: 8/14/1869, D: 3/22/1934, Dixon A. Gates, B: 4/17/1870, D: 7/23/1933, Mabel B. Gates, B: 5/12/1873 D: 3/20/1911, Thomas L. Gates, B: 3/28/1875, D: 7/05/1960, Robert Gates, B: 10/5/1877 D: 12/12/1965, Melville W. Gates, B: 5/1883, D: Unknown

Orin F. Davis, B: 10/15/1854 D: 9/12/1922, Spouse: Sarah Ellen Curler, B: Abt. 1858, D: 5/3/1884, Children: Orin H. Davis, B: 2/4/1880 D: 1/15/1953.

Edward Davis, B: Abt. 1857 D: Unknown, Spouse: Unknown, Children: Unknown.

Vickie Owens

Lillian Ann Cole (Grandmother)
B: 1/26/1894 D: 9/16/1962

Married Charley Davis
5/30/1915

Charley Davis B: 3/7/1887 D: 8/8/1975

Both are laid to rest in
Oakhill Cemetery, Colesburg, Iowa

All their children are listed on page 325-326

Picture of Davis family is shown on page 289

Mary Ann Angel Cole (Livingston)
Great Grandmother
B: 8/25/1858 D: 6/25/1925
Married
John Cole
B: 5/2/1857 D: 8/15/1909
Married
Elias Eli Livingston
B: 5/1846 D: 1/6/1926

Children

James William Cole, B: 9/11/1879 D: 11/22/1982, Spouse: Isabelle Parsons, B: 10/30/1885 D: 3/6/ 1955, Children: Grace Cole, B: 9/24/1908 D: 5/23/1990, Susie Cole, B: 6/6/1911 D: 9/1973, Oscar Cole, B: 5/21/1915 D: 11/8/1969, Russell D. Cole, B: 4/21/1918 D: 6/14/1984.

Sarah Ellen Cole Yonkovic, B: 2/23/1884 D: 12/25/1957 Spouse: Perry Parsons, B: Abt. 1875 D: 4/15/1918, Children: James W. Parsons: B: 1/15/1901 D: 8/15/1961, Della M. Parsons, B: Abt. 1907 D: Unknown, Albert L. Parsons, B: Abt. 1911 D: Unknown, Myrtle M. Parsons, B: Abt. 1914 D: Unknown,
Spouse: Joseph Yonkovic, B: Abt. 1880 D: Unknown, Children: Joseph R. Yonkovic, B: Abt. 1920 D: Unknown.

Bert Cole, B: 1/21/1885 D: 1968, Spouse: Jessie Adel Parsons, B:11/5/1889 D: 2/17/1955, Children: Bertha Cole, B: 10/2/1907 D: 5/3/1993, John William Cole, B: 7/22/1909 D: 8/5/1998, Arthur Cole, B: 9/23/1911 D: 9/28/1990, Blanche May Cole, B:5/22/1916D: 11/4/1933, Verna Cole, B: 7/13/1920 D: 1/11/1981, Martha Cole, B: Abt. 1923 D: 8/12/1984

Alta Cole Bolsinger, B: 2/8/1888 D: 5/14/1977, Spouse: Joseph F. Bolsinger, B: 6/6/1881 D: 1/27/1971, Children: Louis Bolsinger, B: 1905 D: Unknown, Lulu Louisa Bolsinger, B: 7/29/1905 D: 10/27/1992, Clarence Edward Bolsinger, B: 11/25/1907 D:12/4/1982, Florence Bolsinger, B: 4/4/1910 D: 12/16/1968, Elizabeth Lizzie Ann Bolsinger, B: 10/30/1913 D: 1/14/1966, Addie Mae Bolsinger, B: 3/13/1915 D: 10/25/1991, Elmer Bolsinger, B: 3/1/1918 D: 1/5/2011, Blanche Violet Bolsinger, B: 8/15/1920 D: 7/4/2014, Lawrence Bolsinger, B: 4/11/1923 D: 6/14/2004, Gladys Mary Bolsinger, B:5/19/1925 D: 8/28/2001, Glen William Bolsinger, B: 6/19/1927 D: 9/29/2002, Irene Mae Bolsinger, B: 5/5/1930 D: 10/2/2005, Helen Bolsinger, B: Abt. 1933 D: Unknown

Myrtle M. Cole Pirc, B: 11/13/1888 D: 1/4/1971 Spouse: Michael M. Pirc, B: 4/15/1884 D: 11/29/1939, Children: Ralph J Pirc, B: 6/23/1912 D: 10/12/2010, Mary A. Pirc, B: 1/31/1914 D: 8/17/2011, Gerald W. Pirc, B: 8/15/1915 D: 5/1/2007, Laura L Pirc, B: 6/17/1917 D: 10/5/1935, Francis Peter Pirc, B: 8/29/1929 D: 7/28/2010

Frederick Cole, B: 10/20/1890 D: 7/8/1963 Spouse: Anna Mae Bloodworth, B: 1/13/1893 D: 10/22/1961, Children: Boyce Cole, B: Abt. 1914 D: 1940, William Cole, B: 3/25/1916 D: 10/6/1989, Ralph Cole, B: 6/30/1918 D: 5/9/1986,
Irvin Cole, B:9/28/1920, D:10/17/1987 Elmer Cole, B: 12/21/1922 D: 9/19/1989, Vern Cole, B:6/20/1925 D: 6/13/1988, Francis "Pete" Cole, B: 5/20/1934 D: 4/16/2006, Spouse: Florence Davis, B: Unknown D: 2/12/1915, Children: George Cole, B: 10/15/1911, D: Unknown, Mary Ann Cole, B: 1/7/1913 D: 2/19/1990

Michael Henry "Mike" Cole, B: 10/8/1893 D: 9/11/1977, Spouse: Ada "Addie" Chambers, B: 11/15/1897 D: 4/2/1924, Children: Frank Cole, B: 11/23/1915 D: 2/22/1989, Merton Cole, B:1/20/1917 D: 2/6/1999

Lillian Ann Cole-All information can be seen on pages 325-326

Joseph Cole, B: 10/19/1897 D: 9/22/1979
Spouse: Alice Bolsinger, B: 8/2/1897 D: 5/3/1922,
Children: Charles Cole, B: 1917 D: 1917, No other known wives or children at this time.

Robert Cole, B: 5/2/1904 D: 12/1951, Spouse: Martha Bolsinger, B: Abt. 1908 D: Abt. 1928 Children: Lloyd Cole, Birth and Death Unknown.

Vickie Owens

Sarah E. Waymer Angel
Great Great Grandmother
B: Abt. 1841-D: Abt. 1870

Married John E. Angel
B: 9/15/1837 D: 5/30/1917

Children

Mary Ann Angel Cole (Livingston) All information for Mary Ann can be seen on pages 335-337

Parmelia Jane Angel, B:8/28/1863 D: 7/16/1948
Spouse: Charles Wesley Cole, B: 7/6/1863 D: 7/16/1941, Children: Elmer G. Cole B: 8/4/1883 D: 3/1/1957, LeRoy Cole, B: 12/8/1887 D: 1961, Albert Cole, B: 5/21/1890 D: 1960, Earnest Edward Cole, B: 12/19/1891 D: 10/27/1962, Blanche Cole, B: 5/10/1896 D: 10/7/1914,

Amaly Angel, B: Abt. 1864, D: Unknown
Spouse and Children: Unknown

Martha "Mattie" Ellen Angel
B: 12/3/1865 D: 6/9/1949
Spouse: Frank Ferry, B: 3/1864 D: 1940
Children: Ray Ferry, B: 4/3/1890 D: 3/24/1909
Roy Ferry, B: 8/5/1891 D: 8/13/1978, Ralph Clifford Ferry, B:4/7/1905, D: 12/1976

James W. Angel, B: 8/11/1868, D: 6/5/1934 Spouse: Nellie Jane Clendennen, B: 8/15/1872 D: 7/18/1933, No Children Listed

George Washington Angel, B: 5/01/1871 D: 4/16/1945, Spouse: Nora Ann Corson, B: 6/8/1880 D: 11/3/1930 Children: John McKinley Angel, B: 10/25/1896 D: 1/2/1967,
Florence Mae Angel, B:10/26/1899 D: 9/1/1973,
Gladys G. Angel, B: 5/21/1901 D: 11/17/1990, Ferne L. Angel, B: 11/11/1903 D:10/22/1969, Walter Carlton Angel, B: 7/20/1906 D: 10/25/1968, Spouse: Rose Viola Brooks, B: 5/22/1883 D: 4/14/1945

Elizabeth Silbagh Angel
2nd Wife to John E. Angel
B: 4/6/1847 D: 4/12/1918
Married John E Angel

Children

Amma Silbagh, B: Abt. 1866 D: Unknown,
Spouse: Peter A. Collins Birth and Death Unknown, Children: Unknown

Many Silbagh, B: Abt. 1868 D: Unknown
Spouse: Unknown, Children: Unknown

Clary Silbagh, B: Abt. 1870 D: 8/6/1921
Spouse: Peter Anderson Collins, B: 6/3/1860
D: 3/19/1930, Children: William "Will" Collins, B: 6/30/1881
D: 3/14/1950, Merty Jean Collins, B: 11/19/1883 D: 12/4/1883,
Clara Ellen Collins, B: 12/17/1884, D: 3/18/1957
Nellie Caroline Collins, B: 4/12/1887 D: 1/12/1958,
Jay Merle Collins, B: 10/27/1889 D: 11/4/1903, John Collins, B:
1892 D: Unknown, M O Clifton Collins, B:4/8/1892 D: 6/6/1964,
Orvis Benjamin Collins, B: 9/28/1894 D: 3/13/1963,
Minnie H. Collins, B: 8/5/1896 D: 11/22/1971,
Charles Collins, B: 12/1899 D: 10/9/1899,
Sarah L. Collins B:11/13/1901 D:12/29/1930
 Lillian May Collins Nelson, B: 8/28/1904 D: 1/16/1973, Earl
Hector Collins, B: 12/28/1907 D: 12/9/1970, Ray Anderson
Collins, B: 11/12/1909 D: 6/21/1994

Benjamin Silbagh, B: Abt. 1878 D: 1/1968
Spouse: Unknown Children: Unknown.

Ella Violet Angel, B: 8/5/1889 D: 9/22/1966
Spouse: Reuben M. Good, B: 6/1877 D: Children Unknown

I have researched the genealogy to the best of my knowledge. I hope everyone who reads this book enjoys it as much as I have enjoyed piecing it together.

Best wishes to everyone in your life journey

The Final Journey

In May of 2016 my grandson took me to the cabin. It had been forty years since I was last there. We walked the long and winding path to get there. It was a beautiful, memorable experience for both of us. It was his first time there. He always heard Nana talk about the cabin, but wondered how true my stories really were. He got to experience it firsthand. The unimaginable, beautiful place that is now weathered. My roots are still there. My grandparents Old Log Cabin and the long and winding path to get there.

Vickie Owens

The Whispering Pines

The Old Log Cabin
Stands Alone
Weathered Roots

Made in the USA
Las Vegas, NV
10 May 2021